MW00413430

YOUR UNLIMITED LIFE

BREAKING HABITS THAT HOLD YOU BACK

DR. CASEY TREAT

Unless otherwise indicated, all Scripture quotations are taken from The New King James Version of the Bible. Copyright (c) 1979, 1980, 1982, Thomas Nelson, Inc., Publishers.

The Scripture quotations marked AMP is taken from The Amplified Bible, New Testament. Copyright (c) 1958, 1987 by The Lockman Foundation, La Habra, California.

The Scripture quotations marked KJV are taken from The King James Version of the Bible.

Your Unlimited Life: Breaking Habits that Hold You Back
Previously printed as Pulling Down Strongholds and Breaking Old Habits
ISBN - 13: 978-1456586799
ISBN - 10: 1456586793
Copyright (c) 1998 by Casey Treat
2nd Edition, 2011
Christian Faith Center
PO Box 98800
Seattle, WA 98198

Printed in the United States of America. All rights reserved under International Copyright Law. Contents and/or cover may not be reproduced in whole or in part in any form without the express written consent of the Publisher.

Cover Design: JAK Studios

CONTENTS

INTRODUCTION

I'm so excited that you have this book. I believe you will read words of truth in the next pages that will change your life. Each chapter is bathed in prayer and full of the scriptures. *"The Word of God is alive and powerful"* (Hebrew 4:12).

You will probably be angry with me in just a few pages but in a few more you may love me (again). We all believe we need to change to be like Jesus. None of us are there, we have not arrived, we are all on our way to God's perfect will; but change does not come easy. Renewal is a process of awareness, repentance, growing and changing. When we are *"transformed by the renewing of our mind"* (Romans 12:2), we find God's "perfect will." But talking about it, believing in it and actually doing it will set us apart.

I hope to inspire, inform and encourage you to renewal. To overcome the things that have kept you from your best life and lift you to God's plan for your future. God's thoughts toward you are good, He sees a bright future for you (Jeremiah 29:11).

As you walk with Him and experience renewal you will enter that blessed life.

Each chapter will help you understand why certain things have happened in your life and how to get through them. I'm praying that the power of God's Word will take you through and the truth will make you free.

Not only is the Word the foundation and a rock that will never fail, I am sharing with you truths that I have used and am using now. This stuff works. We are *"predestined to be conformed to the image of Jesus"* (Romans 8:29). We aren't there yet, so let's keep renewing our mind and our life.

Proverbs tell us *"For as a man thinketh in his heart, so is he"* (Proverbs 23:7). If you can change one thought or belief you can change your life. It's the things that seem insignificant that get us to the place in life we are now. To get to a new place will take new thoughts. You can do it. The renewed mind brings about your unlimited life.

CASEY TREAT

1

FIRST STEPS TO CHANGE

As a born-again believer, you can only become all God has designed you to be by becoming *renewed in the knowledge of God.* Maturity, success, and enjoyment as a Christian will only come as you are renewed in knowledge after the image of the One who created you.

Spiritually, you become a new person the moment you are born again, and then the process begins. You must learn to set your mind on things above -- on the principles of God, found in His Word. Setting your mind on things above does not mean we should be thinking about heaven all day long. He wants us to set our minds on the principles, on the way of thinking, and on the spiritual thoughts that come from heaven.

We will fail to become successful, fulfilled, and overcoming Christians if we never begin the process of renewing our minds in the knowledge of God. If we fail to take off the old man - the old habits of our carnal nature and put away that old lifestyle - and put on the new man, who is created in the image and like-ness of God, we will never reach the highest level of living God desires for us. Imagine altering your spiritual eternity but never altering your earthly existence because you were unwilling to change your thoughts! God wants more for His children and He makes it easy if we are willing.

In Colossians, chapter 3, Paul talks about setting our minds on "things above" once we are born again:

> *If then you were raised with Christ, seek those things which are above, where Christ is, sitting at the right hand of God. Set your mind on things above, not on things on the earth. For you died, and your life is hidden with Christ in God.*
>
> Colossians 3:1-3

Paul is saying, "If you are born again, the next step is to set your mind in the right place." If you are risen with Christ, seek those things which are above and set your mind on them -- not on the things of the earth.

> *When Christ who is our life appears, then you also will appear with Him in glory. Therefore* [because you are a Christian and you are "in Christ"] *put to death your members that are on the earth: fornication, uncleanness, passion, evil desire, and covetousness, which is idolatry. Because of these things the wrath of God is coming upon the sons of disobedience, in which you yourselves once walked when you lived in them. But now you yourselves are to put off all these: anger, wrath, malice, blasphemy, and filthy language out of your mouth. Do not lie to one another, since you have put off the old man with his deeds, and have put on the new man who is renewed in knowledge according to the image of Him who created him, where there is neither Greek nor Jew, circumcised nor*

uncircumcised, barbarian, Scythian, slave nor free, but Christ is all and in all.

Colossians 3:4-11

Once you are born of God, the knowledge that you live by (or where you set your mind) is the key to every aspect of your life. As a Christian, the success or failure, fulfillment or lack of fulfillment, enjoyment or lack of enjoyment, blessing or lack of blessing you experience, is dependent upon *where you set your mind* - whether you are renewed in the knowledge of God or not. I hope at this point you are beginning to understand the importance of your thoughts.

RENEWAL TRUTH

The Word of Christ dwells

in me richly in all wisdom.

(Colossians 3:16)

GOD GAVE MAN THE POWER OF CHOICE

God created man with two exclusively human, very powerful tools: a sovereign will and the ability to think through the processes of life. If we don't use our will and our mental ability properly, we will not rise to the level of life that God created for us to enjoy. God will not determine our will or use our mental ability for us. He created us in His likeness and image, with the freedom to make the necessary choices to create our own individual lives.

If you were a monkey, He would have put within you the instincts that would control your life, and you wouldn't have any choices to make outside of those instinctual barriers. If you were a dog, God would have programmed you to do what He wanted you to do. If you were a bird, when the right time came, you would head south whether you ever thought about it or not. But, the good news is, you are not an animal!

No matter how hard scientists work to prove that we are part of the animal kingdom, they will never find the missing link. We were created in the likeness and image of God, with an open mind, the ability to choose, and the ability to think. We must use these predisposed rights biblically, so that we will find our place in God where our life will satisfy and fulfill us.

CHOOSE LIFE!

> *I call heaven and earth as witnesses today against you, that I have set before you life and death, blessing and cursing; therefore choose life, that both you and your descendants may live.*
>
> Deuteronomy 30:19

The Bible says that when we stand before God - either after death or after the rapture of the Church - we will give an account of our lives. We cannot give an account for something that we were not in charge of or that we did not have control over. We will give an account of our lives, which is a summation of the choices we made. To say that we were a victim, or that what we did was not our fault, is to deny the reality of the Word of God. God sets before us life and death and He says, *"Choose life."*

As a young man who had already messed things up, created all kinds of problems, who was flooded in misery and depressed about life in general, when someone told me I could change, I sought after that change. I earnestly desired a life that gave me the power to grow and the means to do it.

"You mean I can do something about my life?" Yes! "You mean my life doesn't have to be like this?" No! "You mean I'm not just set on a course deemed by fate?" No! There is no such thing as fate. You don't have to accept anything you don't want to accept; God gave you the power to choose! You can break that bad habit and start living the life God designed for you.

I got motivated. Within a few short years I turned things around in my life because of learning this truth. God created me in His image and likeness, and He gave me the power of choice. My prayer for you is that you grasp this concept and apply it to your life today.

RENEWAL TRUTH

Because I am created in the image and likeness of God,
I have the power to choose life. I choose life!
(Genesis 1:26; Deuteronomy 30:19)

Now, more than thirty years later, I'm still looking for areas in my life where I can make changes. I'm looking for a mountain to which I will say, "I'll climb you." I'm looking at aspects of my life where I can say, "I'll take charge of you. I'll discipline you. I'll overcome that limitation. I'll turn that negative habit around. I will deal with that circumstance." Where you set your mind will control how you live your life. I am continually looking for areas where the choices I make will set the course of my life and put me on the path God has set for me. Seeing the continual increase in my life has allowed me to remain faithful to this process. Every year I am amazed at how my choices to change my thoughts inadvertently change my surroundings and bring increase to my life.

The heart is made up of the spirit and the soul, which is the birthing place of new things and the launching pad for your life. Out of it, you create all the good and bad things that happen in your life.

Sometimes we like to *mystify* or *spiritualize* biblical ideals to the point where we don't feel responsible to practice them because we don't really understand them. How often have you been asked over Sunday lunch how amazing the sermon was, to which you quickly offer your praises? However, you may have already forgotten the teaching and subconsciously decided it will never become a practical part of your daily life.

Since it was so cool, so deep and you feel blessed, why didn't you change anything? That's why we like to talk about the Antichrist, the rapture, and the tribulation. Those topics are really cool and spiritual, but you don't have to do anything. However, when you study the Word, *it's not that mystical, nor does it have to be endlessly deep*. It is very practical with realistic usages.

Man Is Known By His Fruit

In Matthew 12:33 Jesus says, ***"Either make the tree good and*** *its fruit good, or else make the tree bad and its fruit bad; for a tree is known by its fruit."* You can't change the fruit on a tree. An apple tree will not produce pears and pear trees can't produce peaches, but you *can* change the fruit in *your* life by starting to work on the tree itself. This book will help you uproot and replant so that you can have the fruit you desire.

RENEWAL TRUTH

I choose to bear good fruit for God's Kingdom.

(John 15:8)

Jesus used the tree to describe human life. *Unlike people, plants and animals can't change.* They can't renew their minds or choose the way they will produce. They are planted with one purpose and that purpose cannot be altered. People continue trying to keep lions in their houses like domestic kitties. When the lion lashes out, the owner is shocked and confused. The lion is simply doing what comes naturally to him. The human mind is not like that of any other living thing because it has the power to change.

It is all too common for people to try and change the behavior of animals. Like a farmer who tries to make a pig his indoor pet. As soon as the pig has a chance, he will go to the mud. No matter how clean and shiny the pig is, he is still a pig, and he is drawn to his natural habitat - the pigsty.

And so it is that you can't change what has been bred into the natural world. You can't change the fruit of the tree. However, you can change the tree of your life. Jesus says to make the tree good and its fruit good, or make the tree bad and its fruit bad. You make the choice. It's up to you. It is your decision. Set your mind where you want it, and it will decide the kind of life you lead, but the tree (your life) will be known by its fruit. Think of each renewed thought as a new root in your life that is changing the fruit on the tree, soon to harvest the life you desire.

In our secular perspective of things, we don't read, "Make the tree good and its fruit good." We read, "Make the *fruit* good." We want to skip the monotonous discipline of changing the root of the "tree" part and get to the increase! Let's get right to the "fruit." We don't want to work on ourselves but rather just want the benefits and want them now. So when we advertise how to be successful, how to achieve in life, or how to get out of debt, we simply advertise the benefits. No one advertises the discipline, the renewing of the mind, or the working out of this process.

Jesus didn't say to go after the fruit. He said to change the tree, and then the good fruit would come automatically. Make the tree good by working on the roots. Get your mind right. Get your soul right. Get your spirit right. Get your heart right. Then the fruit will be right. Your unlimited life lies right past this up-rooting and replanting process.

In Matthew 12:34, Jesus says, ***"Brood of vipers! How can you, being evil, speak good things? For out of the abundance of the heart the mouth speaks."***

Notice, the condition of the fruit of your life is dependent on what's going on in your heart, and what is going on in your heart is coming out of your mouth. If your heart is good, then good will come out of your mouth. The Lord is trying to get us to understand - the right heart produces the right fruit.

Then He sums it up in verse 35: *"A good man out of the good treasure of his heart brings forth good things, and an evil man out of the evil treasure brings forth evil things."* So whatever is coming out of your mouth - good or bad, rich or poor, happy or sad, big or small - is coming forth from your heart.

We have been programmed to wait for circumstances to change so we can be happy. That's the "victim mentality." The victim believes that everyone else must change in order for me to find my own happiness. Everybody and everything could change yet the victim still wouldn't be happy. The victim never changes because they think the problem lies elsewhere beyond themselves, when, in fact, it's their heart that is the issue. Jesus says when you change in your heart, you will change the fruit of your life.

RENEWAL TRUTH

Create in me a clean heart, O God.

(Psalm 51:10)

Hebrews 4:12 says:

For the word of God is living and powerful, and sharper than any two-edged sword, piercing even to the division of soul and spirit, and of joints and marrow, and is a discerner of the thoughts and intents of the heart.

What does the *soul* and *spirit* do? How do they work? What are their roles? The soul includes the mind, will, and emotions. It's a connector or a joint between the spirit of man and the natural world. Everything that comes to your spirit has to get in your head somehow. It is through your soul that it is united with your spirit so you can use it, say it, and practice it. This is dangerous, because any time you get something in your spirit, you have to run it through your mind. If your mind isn't right, you will twist it. We hear a clear word from God in our spirit, but by the time we interpret it with our mind, we can make it into something completely different. So the connection has to be good. The soul has to be right and we must continually feed spiritual truths from the Word into our mind.

Marrow is where the body creates blood. You've heard of people needing a bone marrow transplant because of a blood disease, cancer, or some other problem. The marrow is a producer or a life force. It's where the blood is created, and the blood is the life of the body.

THE THOUGHTS AND INTENTS OF THE HEART

Thoughts are the basic elements in your soul, and the intents are the basic elements of your spirit. So we've got soul and spirit, joints and marrow, and thoughts and intents. All of these are of the heart. If we get our spirit and soul, joints and marrow, and the thoughts and intents right by the Word of God, then we are going to have a good heart.

Remember Jesus' words from Matthew 12:34-35: *"...out of the abundance of the heart the mouth speaks. A good man out of the good treasure of his heart brings forth good things, and an evil man out of the evil treasure brings forth evil things."*

If your heart has a poor connection, wrong thoughts, you will find yourself struggling to make the growth you want to see in your life. You won't make it. You won't get the fruit that you are looking, praying, and working for. The tree won't produce good fruit because the heart is where the key issue lies and it's unhealthy. It all started with wrong thinking.

God's Word is the key to getting your heart right. The Word of God is the sharp, two-edged sword that cuts out the stuff you don't want and sharpens the things you do want. The Word works in the heart to make it healthy and fruitful. Mark 4 talks about the sower sowing the Word. Where did he sow it? In the heart. So when the heart is right, your life will produce good and when your heart isn't right, your life will be a struggle.

When you become a Christian, your spirit is born again. Your spirit is recreated and you become a new person in Christ. You are one with the Spirit of God with direct access and authority to use His power that is now alive in you. He that is joined to the Lord is one spirit with Him. But Paul says the mind needs some work done on it. Since you now have access to the greatest power, God, you are going to need to obey Paul and get your mind in alignment with what your spirit man is now yearning for. Breaking habits that hold you back starts by changing the negative thoughts that drive your life.

RENEWAL TRUTH

I am a new creature in Christ Jesus.
Old things have passed away, and the new has come.
(2 Corinthians 5:17)

I wish we could get the mind born again and changed instantly. It could be like the old movie Matrix; we could be like Neo, hooking our mind up and getting a renewed mind download! Too bad it is not that easy. "Just do it, Lord! Go ahead, I give You permission." But the Lord says, "You are made like Me, so I can't change your soul. I can recreate your spirit, but I can't change your soul. You have to do that."

So how do we do it? Go back to Colossians 3:2: *"Set your mind on things above."* Then, *"be renewed in knowledge according to the image of* [Jesus]*"* (v. 10). Begin to set your mind on the right things. Begin to change the way you think so you can think like Jesus thinks.

In every circumstance of life, I ask myself, "What would Jesus think about this? How would He respond to this situation? Am I being renewed in knowledge after the image of the One who created me?"

This is why it is so important that we know the Word. I don't want to make up my own interpretation of what Jesus would do. Assuming certain choices as the moral compass to live by is vastly different than studying the Word and knowing the moral compass to live by. I want to base my thinking on the Word of God. That's how we learn what Jesus would do. Jesus is the Word made flesh. If you know the Word, you will know the Lord. If you don't know the Word, you won't know the Lord.

By getting the Word working in your heart, you will learn how to be renewed in the knowledge of Jesus. This is what Christian growth is all about. This is how you break habits, change your life and your thoughts, so that you can have an unlimited life.

You would think this would be an easily understood and well-known truth, but it isn't. As our television program goes out across the world, the most common response we get to this teaching is, "We've never heard this before." Now, maybe what they are saying is that their pastor taught it or they've heard about it, but it never became clear to them. But the bottom line remains; it is a truth that we must learn and apply to our lives daily.

We all know people who have never understood what it is to get their heart right and get their mind renewed so they can be the people God created them to be. They are waiting on the sovereign will of God. They are wondering why God allowed this or that. They hear the teaching but they refuse to take responsibility for their mind and their life. The truth is, what is in their life came out of their heart, but they can't see it. They can't grasp it because they have never understood that out of the heart comes our way of thinking, our way of speaking, and the fruit of our life. What is in your heart comes out of your mouth, and forms your life.

RENEWAL TRUTH

I receive the abundant life that Jesus has come to give me, and I reject the stealing, killing, and destroying which the devil has been sent to do. I am a child of God, and His blessings are overtaking me.

(John 10:10)

Another example of the power of the human heart is seen when we are in emergency circumstances. Studies have been done of people's responses in life and death situations. You would think that people in a life and death situation would call out to God: "Lord, forgive me. I should have gotten saved a long time ago. I'm sorry I didn't. I am giving You my life right now." But this rarely happens.

When people are afraid, stressed, or in a life and death situation, whatever is in their heart will come out. Usually, if they are of the world, it's cursing, anger, and bitterness. For the Christian we daily renew our thinking so when emergency strikes, it's praise, prayer, and faith. You can't wait until the end of your life to get right. You've got to work on your heart day by day, because at the end, whatever is in you will control you. Out of the abundance of your heart you will speak.

It may be valuable to give ourselves a little grace when anger, frustration, or the like comes out. Yet it is time we take responsibility for what is being spoken out of the mouth. We need to realize that if it weren't in the core of our minds, it would not come out.

I'm not talking about covering it up, learning how to control your tongue, and learning how to stuff it down deeper. This book is not designed to teach mind over matter, or burying old pains that have created your world today. Your reality should be that it couldn't come out because it's not in your heart. You have to take responsibility to get your heart right and it starts by literally replacing one thought with another.

As parents we all have experienced changing dirty diapers. Step one is to take off the old, then step two, replace the diaper with a clean one. When your puppy makes a mess in the corner you don't just put a newspaper over it, you fully wipe it clean. As we fill our hearts with God's Word we are also removing the negatives that have so limited our lives and putting in God's best.

Most people make a good confession when they think about it: "I believe I am healed. I believe all of my needs are met. God is prospering my business. God is blessing me. My steps are ordered of the Lord." But when they are in casual conversation throughout the day the confessions that spoke and read out loud take a backseat to the overwhelming reality of the moment and they say things like, "I don't know what I'm going to do. We are going broke. My back is killing me."

RENEWAL TRUTH
Death and life are in the
power of my tongue.
I will speak life.
(Proverbs 18:21)

When you think about it, you make a good confession, but when you're not thinking about it, all that negativity in your heart comes out. That is what is killing you, keeping the pain in you, frustrating you, and keeping the stint on your life. Each of us must become responsible for the condition of our hearts and make sure that the only thing that comes out is "good" fruit.

Setting your mind on God's Word is the beginning to your ultimate life. It is the essential ingredient to God's best for you. If you receive this message alone, this book would be deemed a success. Understand the principle of the tree bringing forth fruit. Setting your mind on God's Word is like uprooting the rotten tree and planting a new one. You can do it - your unlimited life awaits you.

Personal Application of Renewal Truths

1. I set my mind on "things above" by: _____

   _____

   _____

   _____

2. I put off the old man and his evil deeds and put on the new man by (see Colossians 3:10): _____

   _____

   _____

   _____

3. Unlike animals, God created man with the ability to make choices. According to Deuteronomy 30:19, God has set before me life and death, blessing and cursing. Then He says, "_____ "
   I choose life!

4. Good fruit will be produced in my life by: _____

   _____

   _____

   _____

   _____

   _____

   _____

5. To me, a "victim mentality" means: _____

_____

_____

_____

6. My soul is made up of:

    a. _____

    b. _____

    c. _____

7. I am removing the "negatives" out of my heart and mind, and I am replacing them with "positives" that agree with God's Word by (3 examples):

_____

_____

_____

_____

_____

_____

_____

_____

_____

_____

_____

_____

2

YOUR HEART CONDITION

In Matthew 15:2 the Pharisees asked Jesus, *"Why do Your disciples transgress the tradition of the elders? For they do not wash their hands when they eat bread."*

That ticked Jesus off! He began to confront them and ended up calling them hypocrites. His wrath serves to highlight the importance of the situation and brings light to the reality of the power of the mouth.

Jesus said to them, *"Not what goes into the mouth defiles a man; but what comes out of the mouth, this defiles a man"* (v. 11). The disciples said to Jesus, *"Do You know that the Pharisees were offended by Your message today?"* (v. 12). Then, in verse 15, Peter said to Jesus, "Explain this parable to us." Jesus responded:

> *Are you also still without understanding? Do you not yet understand that whatever enters the mouth goes into the stomach and is eliminated? But those things which proceed out of the mouth come from the heart, and they defile a man. For out of the heart proceed evil thoughts.*
>
> Matthew 15:16-19

Notice, that which can defile your life and comes out of the heart are your *thoughts*. Some of us have been taught that the heart is synonymous with the spirit and it is separate from your mind or soul. But here we recognize what's going on in your thinking is an integral part of what is going on in your heart and therefore must acknowledge the connection and unity therein. I am convinced from Scripture that your heart is made up of spirit and soul. The inner man is your heart; spirit and soul, and your heart includes your thoughts. If your thoughts aren't right, your heart isn't right.

Have you ever heard someone say, "He has a good heart but a bad temper," or "that wasn't like her to say that; she means well"? In reality, although socially we have accepted those statements, they contradict the Bible. If you have bad thoughts, they are coming out of your heart.

> *For out of the heart proceed evil thoughts, murders, adulteries, fornications, thefts, false witness, and blasphemies. These are the things which defile a man, but to eat with unwashed hands does not defile a man.*
>
> Matthew 15:19-20

Religion, tradition, and the world inevitably force you to focus on all the wrong priorities. Even in church we see the power of the enemy trying to derail our thoughts and fill our mind with distractions that hold no eternal value. If you allow your thoughts to control you, you will become concerned with things like what kind of car the preacher drives, who is serving communion, or the attire of the praise team, rather than the condition of the hearts of those receiving communion, the passion of the praise team desperately trying to lead you in worship, or the level of sacrifice the pastor has given in order to be your spiritual authority. All the things that God does not care about such as religion, traditions, and the world have stolen people's focus.

God cares about the condition of the heart because that is where the fruit and the productivity of your life will originate. What goes on in the heart of man is relevant because out of it springs the quality of life. A right heart will attract God's best to you, while a wrong heart will attract trouble and problems. Either you will walk in the blessings and enjoy all God has for you, or you will keep bringing forth trouble.

RENEWAL TRUTH

Search me, O God, and know my heart:

try me, and know my thoughts.

(Psalm 139:23 KJV)

If you set your mind on things above and are renewed in knowledge after the image of Jesus, you will stay on course with God's destiny for you.

STRUGGLE, STRUGGLE, STRUGGLE!

Why do many Christians go through divorce? Go bankrupt? Stay sick? Get angry? Lie? We are supposed to be delivered from all of these problems, so why are they still going on? The answer is though we are saved, we haven't set our minds on things above and we haven't gotten our hearts right. As I said in the first chapter, it is because the tree is still rotten and it needs to be uprooted and a new tree needs to be planted.

Why do many Christians struggle with their weight? Is it your hormones and your metabolism? Why do you fight in your marriage? Why can't some get their children to obey, catch up on their financial obligations and get out of debt? The good man out of the good treasure of the heart brings forth good things, but the poor man out of the poor treasure of his heart keeps bringing forth poverty. What are we to do? We must get the heart right.

Some people say, "I love God. I am sincere. I'm telling you the truth, Pastor, my heart is right." In that sense the heart is right, but what thoughts are going on in the heart? It's not about being sincere or being a good person. It's about knowing what's going on with your thoughts. And now that you are aware, the power to change is available.

There are people who can't receive this teaching because they don't have a clue what is going on in their head. If you don't have some awareness of what is happening in you, you can't even begin to understand this teaching. It takes honesty and openness to understand and then apply this teaching in your life.

When I first got saved, my mentor, Julius Young, would say to me, "Casey, you don't even know what is going on in your own head." I wanted to act like I knew everything about the world, yet I was nineteen, fresh off the streets, and had memorized maybe three Bible verses. He said, "You not only don't know the world, you don't know yourself." Of course, in my adolescence I thought I knew everything and explained to him in my freshly sober state that I was fully aware of my environment. He responded, "You are completely unaware. You've got wrong thoughts and wrong attitudes so deeply imbedded in you and this process of change is going to be just that, a process."

Do you ever catch yourself mad about something and you say, "Why did I get mad?" "What set me off today?" That's where you are unaware. Do you ever catch yourself in the refrigerator, choking down about 9,000 calories, and you are thinking, "My God, why am I doing this?" Or, rationalizing one more day of cigarettes, thinking, "Why do I keep going through this?" Do you catch yourself skipping one more trip to the gym, and you wonder, "Why do I keep neglecting my exercise time?"

You are so unaware of how you are thinking that you are doing things out of habit, and therefore you are not getting the fruit that you want. You keep doing it because you haven't plugged in to how to renew your mind, how to change your heart, or how to take hold of that tree so it starts producing the kind of fruit you desire.

RENEWAL TRUTH

I am swift to hear, slow to speak,

and slow to wrath.

(James 1:19)

LOVING GOD WITH A "RIGHT" MIND

Just remember, out of the heart proceeds thoughts that will either bring blessing or cursing, which will either take you to the will of God or away from the will of God. If we love God with all our heart, it includes having our mind *focused on Him*.

When the Pharisees asked Jesus, *"Which is the great commandment in the law,"* Jesus responded, *"You shall love the Lord your God with all your heart, with all your soul, and with all your mind"* (Matthew 22:36-37). Why did He say that? Because He wanted us to know that loving God doesn't just mean a vain repetition of lip service repeating how much we love Him, then going off and doing our own thing. It means getting our mind right. Jesus said to love God with all your heart, soul, and mind. I'm convinced that Jesus said heart, soul, and mind to emphasize the focus. Nowhere does it say thoughts, words, and good intentions. Rather it says to love Him with your heart, soul, and mind, all three of these elements being of extreme importance.

"With all your heart" means with all your soul, and with all your mind. This means to *set your mind on things above*. It doesn't mean to think about Heaven all day. It means to order your mind based on what God says in His Word.

RENEWAL TRUTH

I am hiding Your Word in my heart, Lord,

so I won't sin against You.

(Psalm 119:11)

Jesus said, *"Love the Lord your God with all your heart, with all your soul, and with all your mind"* (Matthew 22:37). I hear some people say, and I'm sure you have too, "She really loves the Lord, but she just has this sin problem." "He really loves the Lord, but he can't whip the alcohol." "He really loves the Lord, but he just can't separate himself from adultery (or fornication)." "She loves God and is a wonderful person, but she has an anger problem."

The previous statements simply are not possible in their truest form. If you love God with all your heart, that means with your soul and it means your mind is right with God. If your mind is right with God, you won't have an anger problem, a drinking problem, or an adultery problem. You will have the power to control your mind and the audacity to *set your mind on things above*. You won't allow sin to rule your life because your mind is focused on Him.

RENEWAL TRUTH

God keeps me in perfect peace,
because my mind is focused on Him.
(Isaiah 26:3)

"I love God, but I'm afraid." You can't love God and be afraid at the same time, because perfect love casts out fear (1 John 4:18). If you love God with all your heart, soul and mind, your mind is stayed [focused] on Him and you will have perfect peace.

Setting your mind on the right things affects every aspect of life. When you begin to realize what your soul is doing to every aspect of your life, you will stop excusing and rationalizing: "God's will be done. He will do it in His time, and in His time He makes all things beautiful." No, it's when you get your mind focused on Him.

Again, I'm not talking about mind games, mind tricks, and mental-exercises. What I am saying is that biblically, *when your mind is right, your heart will be right.* When you love God with all your heart, things will be right. It's a good tree that produces good fruit. The good tree (person) starts working! The bills get paid, the kids obey, the marriage is fun, and everything happens for good.

RENEWAL TRUTH

God has not given me a spirit of fear,
but He has given me power, love, and a sound mind.

(2 Timothy 1:7)

"But I'm just waiting on the Lord." No, He's waiting on you! He's waiting on you to love Him with all your heart, soul, and mind. Get your mind focused on Him, and perfect peace will flow in your life.

SANCTIFIED BY THE WORD

3 John 2 says, *"Beloved, I pray that you may prosper in all things and be in health, just as your soul prospers."* The King James Version of this verse says, *"Beloved, I wish above all things that thou mayest prosper and be in health, even as thy soul prospereth."*

I believe this verse shows us several things. First, John wouldn't pray for you to prosper and be in health and record it in Holy Scripture if it wasn't God's will. Second, the key to your prosperity "in all things" and being in health is the *well-being of your soul.*

How does the soul prosper? Verse 3 holds the answer: *"For I rejoiced greatly when brethren came and testified of the truth that is in you, just as you walk in the truth."* The truth is the

Word of God.

In John 17:17 Jesus said, *"Sanctify them by Your truth. Your Word is truth."* The Word is a sharp, two-edged sword that affects the heart, spirit, and soul. Truth causes your heart and soul to prosper. When your soul prospers, you will prosper in all things and live in health.

In John 8:31-32 Jesus said, *"If you abide in My word, you are My disciples indeed. And you shall know the truth, and the truth shall make you free."*

As you set your mind on the things of the Word, you will know the truth. Many Christians know more about their doctor and what he says than they do about what God says. They know more about what the lawyer says than what God says. They know more about what the talk show host says than they do about what God says. They know more about what the whole world says than they do about what the Word says.

However, as you get into the Word and you come to know the truth, it will make you free. You will then prosper and be in health, even as your soul prospers.

Keep your mind focused on Jesus and you will have perfect peace. Love God with all your heart, soul, and mind, and all that God has for you will open up to you. Out of your heart you will start bringing forth prosperity because your soul is prospering. As the truth -- God's Word -- takes hold of your spirit and soul, your mind is renewed, your heart is renewed, and you will begin to prosper in your health, finances, family, and everything else.

Personal Application of Renewal Truths

1. To keep from being controlled by wrong thoughts, I will:

   _____

   _____

   _____

   _____

2. I attract God's "best" blessings to me by believing:

   _____

   _____

   _____

3. I focus my mind on God by: _____

   _____

   _____

   _____

4. The prosperity of my spirit and body is proportionate to the prosperity of my: _____

   _____

   _____

5. My soul prospers by (see 3 John 2): _____

   _____

   _____

6. I am sanctified by: _____

   _____

   _____

   _____

7. The truth of God's Word has set me free from:

_____

_____

_____

_____

_____

_____

_____

_____

_____

_____

8. I need the truth of God's Word to set me free from:

_____

_____

_____

_____

_____

_____

_____

_____

_____

_____

_____

_____

_____

_____

_____

_____

_____

_____

3

WHO TOLD YOU?

Let's go back to the book of Genesis and see how God taught Adam and Eve about the importance of aligning their thoughts with His words. At this point, *defilement* wasn't even in their vocabulary; they were perfect in the image of God.

Adam and Eve represented all of us back in the Garden of Eden. They embody the ideal person or the perfect creation God intended for all of humanity. Theologically, we refer to Adam as the federal head of mankind. In other words, what he did has affected all of our lives.

Let's begin in Genesis, chapter 3:

Now the serpent was more cunning than any beast of the field which the Lord God had made. And he said to the woman, "Has God indeed said, `You shall not eat of every tree of the garden?'" And the woman said to the serpent, "We may eat of the fruit of the trees of the garden; but of the fruit of the tree which is in the midst of the garden, God has said, `You shall not eat it, nor shall you touch it, lest you die.'" Then the serpent said to the woman, "You will not surely die. For God knows that in the day you eat of it your eyes will be opened, and you will be like God, knowing good and evil."

So when the woman saw that the tree was good for food, that it was pleasant to the eyes, and a tree desirable to make one wise, she took of its fruit and ate. She also gave to her husband with her, and he ate.

Genesis 3:1-6

Adam was standing there the whole time. I used to believe that Adam was busy naming animals or off somewhere else completely oblivious to what Eve was doing, but no, he was right there the entire time. He allowed the serpent to go on and on, then he ate with Eve.

RENEWAL TRUTH

I'll not be ensnared by the lust of the flesh,
the lust of the eyes, or the pride of life. Instead,
I'll be captivated and motivated by God's Word.

(1 John 2:16)

Verse 7 says, *"Then the eyes of both of them were opened."* Had they been walking around blind? What does "their eyes were opened" mean? It means they had new thoughts they had never had before. They had knowledge they hadn't had previous to this historic event.

The serpent wasn't more powerful, more beautiful, or more authoritative. Scripture says he was *more cunning*. We must realize that the power and authority of the devil and his demonic spirits aren't the problem we face today. It's their cunning maneuvers, lies, trickery, and deceit that get us.

The serpent was cunning and he began to play with Eve's head: *"You will not surely die. For God knows that in the day you eat of it your eyes will be opened, and you will be like God, knowing good and evil"* (Genesis 3:4-5).

Adam and Eve were already like God. They were created in His image and likeness (Genesis 1:26). Eve was deceived by her thoughts because she didn't guard or discipline her mind. She didn't go to her husband and consult him first with the thoughts of doubt that she had started to believe. She didn't approach him and explain the ways in which it sounded interesting and was appealing to her. Nor did Adam stop her and remind her that the words of the serpent weren't true and that they already were like God. Neither one of them stopped the serpent, quoted their Creator God, and neither one of them went to God and asked Him to remind them of the promise that was already theirs.

Adam and Eve let their minds get caught up in deception. They believed the lie the devil told them, believing that God probably had been keeping something from them and that there must be more to life.

They let the serpent's lies take rest in their minds. Remember, the lie of the devil is the opposite of the truth of the Word. If the Word brings you truth and the truth makes you free, a lie brings you into bondage and deception and keeps you bound. If a prosperous soul is full of the truth, then a poor soul is full of lies. The devil has no other power but to distort true power, God's Word.

RENEWAL TRUTH

I am prospering in my spirit, soul, and body,

as well as in my relationships and finances,

because I am filled with God's truth.

(Joshua 1:8; Psalm 1:1-3)

EXPOSING SATAN'S LIES

Here's the bottom line for everyone who is struggling: *You are believing the things that the devil said, not what God said.* Here are three examples of the devil's lies:

Lie #1 that will keep you in financial bondage: "*Not everybody has to tithe because tithing is a law and puts people in bondage, and Jesus said we are not to live in bondage.*" The act of giving your tithe is a principle established in the Old Testament and carried over to the New Testament in order to keep a heart of giving, to open your life up for abundance, and to take care of the needs of the church. Tithing is a command (Malachi 3:8-12). You can believe a lie, but I'll believe the Word. Then let's see where you and I are, respectively, as far as our finances are concerned in ten years. The lie will bring bondage, but the truth will bring freedom.

Lie #2 that can keep you sick: "*God doesn't heal everybody.*" You can believe that if you want to, but I'm going to believe the Word. God is no respecter of persons (Acts 10:34). By Jesus' stripes you were already healed (1 Peter 2:24). During my battle with Hepititas C, if I did not capture this lie and push it out of my mind, I would have been deeply destroyed. Rather, I chose to believe that God is a good God and brings healing to all people. The lie brings bondage, while the truth brings freedom.

Lie #3 that can ruin your family: "If my husband doesn't change, I will leave him. God wants me to be happy. If I have to divorce him to be happy, that's what I will do." Scripture (truth) says God hates divorce (Malachi 2:16). It says to love your spouse and submit to one another (Ephesians 5:21-33). You can believe the lie, but I'm going to believe the truth.

The bottom line is: You can be caught up in a lie and as a result be entangled in all kinds of bondage. Or, you can be in agreement with the truth of God's Word and walk in absolute freedom. Being in agreement with the Word is not always easy but it is always the best route to take. It brings clarity and assurance into our hearts.

In Eve's case, the serpent came along and convinced her that God meant otherwise. Eve bought into the lie, so she and Adam ate and their eyes were opened. They began to think things they had never thought before and to know things they had not known previously, and the source of their knowledge was not God. Just because you agree to the world's ways and see things that you did not know before does not mean it is beneficial to your life. It is more important to guard your heart than to seek worldly understanding.

RENEWAL TRUTH

Believing Satan's lies and buying into his deceptions
bring bondage. Believing the truth of
God's Word brings me into absolute freedom.
(Galatians 5:1,13; Psalm 119:45)

GRABBING FOR THE LEAVES!

Genesis 3:7 says that after their eyes were opened, *"...they knew that they were naked; and they sewed fig leaves together and made themselves coverings."* Isn't it interesting that as soon as they thought something that didn't come from God, they wanted to cover themselves and hide?

When you think things that aren't from God, you don't want mom and dad to know. Just like many children learn to lie and cover up things they believe are wrong, in our adult life, we carry these traits over and lie to cover ourselves.

Husbands and wives often do the same thing. They begin to hide and not talk about things. What are you covering? What is it you don't want to share? In a relationship where day after day things are covered up, division will eventually come.

Adam and Eve must have questioned their own foolish behavior at some point and wondered to themselves what they were doing naked in the garden. Who cares? No one else was there. The weather was perfect. The chimpanzees weren't going to give them any trouble. They were the only humans there. But the sin nature is to "cover" when something isn't right.

Then God shows up:

And they heard the sound of the Lord God walking in the garden in the cool of the day, and Adam and his wife hid themselves from the presence of the Lord God among the trees of the garden. Then the Lord God called to Adam and said to him, "Where are you?"

Genesis 3:8-9

When God asks a question, it's not because He doesn't already know the answer. It's because He wants you to think about the answer. He says, "Adam, what are you doing?"

Adam responds, "Nothing."

Adam and Eve's sin opened their minds to thoughts that didn't come from God. Up to this time, their thoughts were undefiled by anything of the world.

RENEWAL TRUTH

I choose to be undefiled by sin,

not because everything

that is hidden will be revealed,

but because I want to be like Jesus.

(Matthew 10:26; 1 John 3:2)

THE "SOURCE" OF YOUR KNOWLEDGE

Adam said, *"I heard Your voice...I was afraid because I was naked; and I hid myself. And He* [God] *said, 'Who told you that you were naked?'"* (Genesis 3:10,11). In other words, "Where did you even come up with that thought?"

Let's go back to chapter 2, verses 16 and 17, where the forbidden tree was identified: *"And the Lord God commanded the man, saying, 'Of every tree of the garden you may freely eat; but of the tree of the knowledge of good and evil you shall not eat, for in the day that you eat of it you shall surely die.'"*

Isn't it interesting that this tree is about *knowledge?* It is about the thoughts of good and evil. Notice, God said it's a tree of the knowledge of *good* as well as evil. In every temptation there are things that are good. The issue isn't that it's good or even that it's evil because God gave them the knowledge of good and evil. The issue is—*where are you getting your knowledge?* That's what the tree represents: the *source* of your thoughts.

God was saying, "I want the *source* of everything you think, everything you believe, and everything in your life to be Me. As long as it's Me, you've got it made in the shade. But the minute you turn to some other source—yourself, the devil, or the world —you are going to have problems and you will lose your relationship with Me. You're going to die spiritually, and then you will have opened the door for curses to come on you." And that's exactly what happened with Adam and Eve.

The key is not what you know, it's how you know it:
- Who told you that you can't get out of debt?
- Who told you that you're not smart?
- Who told you that you can't get a better job?
- Who told you that you can't make more money?
- Who told you that your company can't be bigger than it is?
- Who told you that your husband (or wife) won't change?
- Who told you that you can't be healthy?
- Who told you that you're ugly?
- Who told you that you can't have a good marriage?
- Who told you that you've sinned too much to be forgiven?
- Who told you that you would never own your own home?
- Who told you that you can't be healed?

Begin to question the source of every thought. That was

God's question of Adam: *"Who told you that you were naked?"* (Genesis 3:11).

Don't you think God would have told Adam and Eve about good and evil and talked to them about anything they wanted to know? If Adam had asked God what being naked meant, don't you think God would have told him? The problem was, Adam went to the devil instead of to the Lord.

We want our children to know the difference between good and evil. We will tell them what's going on, both the bad side as well as the good side, but we don't want them to go to the bad side to find out firsthand what is bad. The *source* of their knowledge is the key to their destiny. If they know about good and evil from godly instruction, they will prosper in their soul. But if they know about good and evil because they've been in the gutter and finding its meaning out from the world, they will have hurts, pains, and turmoil that will drag them down for years to come.

RENEWAL TRUTH

God is the source of my knowledge.
In Him, I live and move and have my being.
Obedience to His direction is the key to
the fulfillment of my divine destiny.
(Acts 17:28; 1 Samuel 15:22)

When my sons and my daughter were young, I wanted them to know about sex. I talked to them about sex and they didn't even want to talk about it yet, but there came a day when they were more interested. Recently, my oldest son got married. I hope that I trained him about a healthy sexual relationship progressively as he aged in maturity. I talked to them about it then because I wanted them to get the knowledge of sex from a godly perspective. I didn't want them to get the knowledge of sex from the back seat of a car, from a *Playboy* magazine, or from some other secular humanist health teacher.

Knowledge from worldly sources would have hurt them. The knowledge I gave them about sex was from God's perspective, from God's Word, and that knowledge brought a healthy perception and understanding of physical intimacy in a marriage relationship.

In the past, the church tried to keep people in the dark about sex. We talk about everything but sex from God's perspective. The tree of the knowledge of life is truth and it brings freedom. But the knowledge of good and evil is deceptive, cunning, twisted, and perverted. While there's some good in it, the evil in it will bring bondage.

Most people who are struggling in their sexual relationship are struggling because much of what they think about sex came from the tree of the knowledge of good and evil. It didn't come from the tree of life from God. It came from the world. It doesn't make you evil, but it just means you have some thoughts that are binding you up, holding you back, and keeping you from God's perfect will. This concept of where you attain your knowledge applies to almost every area of our life. Which is why applying these principles is monumental in your walk with God. If we evaluate where the knowledge came from, and the good and bad therein, then we will be able to accurately take out the worldly thoughts and replace them with biblical truths.

If you're struggling with sex, finances, relationships, or with children, you have knowledge that came from the tree of the knowledge of good and evil. You are operating off of thoughts that came from this world rather than from God, and those thoughts will keep you in bondage until you renew your mind with God's Word.

The question is, who told you? Who told you that you can't communicate? Who told you that you're not good at sharing your feelings?

When you start questioning everything the world tells you, you will start getting free. Stop and acknowledge which thoughts came from the devil. Recognize that which came from the tree of the knowledge of good and evil. Shift your thinking to only accepting the thoughts that come from God. Then you will see your soul starting to prosper. Your mind will start to be renewed. You are setting your mind on things above, not on the things of the world, and all of a sudden the blessings of God start coming on you.

RENEWAL TRUTH

I am standing fast in the liberty Christ has provided for me.
I'll not be entangled again with the
bondage of believing Satan's lies.
(Galatians 5:1)

Who told you that you have a temper? Where did you get that thought? Don't believe it. You simply have bad thinking. Your temper isn't any different than anyone else's temper. But, you've got an attitude because of thoughts that somebody from the tree of the knowledge of good and evil put in your mind.

Look at any area of your life where you believe you have a problem and ask yourself, "Where did I get that thought? What thoughts have I been operating from? What thoughts have been controlling me?"

We like to blame Satan for taking our jobs, our spouses, and our health, and certainly he is the source of *all evil*. But don't just blame the *source*. Look at *how you let it come into your life*.

When a mouse is in my house, I know a mother mouse birthed that little critter, but the mother mouse is not my problem. The problem is: *how did he get in my house?* There is a devil and you know he is the ultimate source of every problem, but that's not the real issue. The issue is: *how did the problem get in your life?* If you plug the hole, you don't care how many mother mice are out there! As long as they aren't in your house, the mother mice can do whatever they want to do. When you plug the hole in your life, the devil can do whatever he wants to do but he won't be able to get in! None of his antics will affect you!

RENEWAL TRUTH

Because I am submitted to God,

I resist the enemy and he flees from me.

(James 4:7)

Disciplining the Mind With God's Word

Paul said, *"For though we walk in the flesh, we do not war according to the flesh"* (2 Corinthians 10:3). We live in a fleshly body and a carnal, physical world, but we don't war according to the flesh. In other words, don't make things in the physical world around you the issues that you are struggling with.

In our church, we don't preach about hair and clothes and all that stuff because that's not where the battle is. If you want to color your hair or paint your face, just do what you are going to do. Be modest and reasonable, but that's not the issue. When you get into the fleshly battles and everything becomes a physical issue, you are off track.

When little kids are worried about their physical body, we say to them, "Come on, you're going to grow up. Don't worry. Don't even think about it. Everything is going to be cool! Get your mind educated. Learn to serve God and that won't be a problem."

As adults we need to learn this lesson, because we spend an hour primping our body and two seconds plugging into the Spirit. We have time to shower, shave, paint, color, comb, brush and spray, but we have little or no time to pray. Don't let your fleshly, physical being demand center stage in your life.

For the weapons of our warfare are not carnal [physical, fleshly] *but mighty in God for pulling down strongholds.*

2 Corinthians 10:4

If I stopped right here and started talking about the strong-holds of the devil, you would shout, for most Christians are into this: "Yeah, we need to pull down the strongholds of the devil. We need to speak to the prince of the power of the air and go after the demons in the spirit realm. We need to do warfare and wrestle against principalities and powers." We get all fired up about this stuff, because it's an ethereal [or intangible] thing that doesn't make us look at our practical lives.

Are you a better wife? "No, but I broke the power of the dev-il." Did you pay any bills? "No, but I went into the third heaven." Did you clean your house? "Yeah, I got the spirits out of there." Why don't you just deal with the garbage? We like to talk about the strongholds and spiritual things, but what are they?

2 Corinthians 10:5 says:

> *Casting down arguments* [The King James Version says imaginations] *and every high thing that exalts itself against the knowledge of God, bringing every thought into captivity to the obedience of Christ.*

Paul is not talking about demons. He is talking about argu-ments, imaginations, rationalities, thoughts, and knowledge. These are the strongholds that keep us from winning the war and from being the people God wants us to be. We are dealing with the same thing that we dealt with back in the Garden of Eden. Satan wasn't the problem. Adam opened their minds to the thoughts, deceptions, and lies of the devil. They could have kicked the devil out of the garden with their little pinkies. They could have stepped on the serpent and stomped his head! I mean, they could have roasted him and had their first meal of meat.

Adam and Eve had the authority and dominion of God over every beast of the field. They could have wrung the serpent's neck and had a gourmet dinner, but their heads got in the way. The strongholds that caused them to sin were deception, fleshly ideas, and lies. These strongholds removed them from the blessing of God and got them kicked out of the Garden of Eden.

Although Satan is the father of all lies (John 8:44), and this may shock you but, ultimately he and his demons are not your problem because he is already defeated through Jesus' cross. The way you win the war over his strongholds is by getting your mind renewed to the Word of God and not buying into his lies and deceptions; not allowing arguments and worldly knowledge to be exalted against the knowledge of God.

When you get your mind disciplined with the Word, you will win every war! That is where you will find freedom, abundant life, and the blessings of God. By being transformed by the renewing of your mind with God's Word, you will find God's perfect will.

RENEWAL TRUTH
God always causes me to triumph in Christ.
(2 Corinthians 2:14)

When revival hits, if your mind is still all messed up, it won't have a great lasting impact upon your life. Many of us have gone to conferences, services, and meetings where we got in the glory cloud. Glory balls were busted over our heads, and we fell out under the power of God. We laughed until our stomachs hurt. Or simply truly felt a touch from God. Then we went home and the wife still hates the husband, the kids are still rebelling, the bills still aren't paid, and we are still thirty-five pounds overweight. We look in the mirror and we still feel ugly. We then think that we must quickly go back to the glory balls, back to the cloud, back to the anointing, and have the evangelist pray for us again!

Thank God for the miracles and for His presence, but if we aren't renewing our minds with God's Word, nothing is going to change. If we aren't renewing our minds with God's Word, we will never win the war.

I can cast the devil out of someone who needs deliverance, but I cannot cast out his or her thoughts, rationales, and imaginations. Demons will obey me, but your negative thinking won't. That's why you can pray against these things and rebuke them, but there will be no lasting change until you renew your mind to God's Word.

Case in point: smoking. Most people start smoking because they are trying to look cool. Then they find out that cigarettes are killing them, so they want to quit. So, how are they going to quit? Rebuke a nicotine demon, right? Brother So-and-so prays and casts out a nicotine demon, but the next morning your cup of coffee isn't right without a cigarette. Or, you can't go back to work after lunch without a cigarette. Or, you go all day without a cigarette, then after dinner when you have your latte, you think, "After all day I deserve a cigarette. Brother So-and-so cast a demon out of me and he's a man of God, a man of authority. How come I'm thinking about cigarettes again?"

Some people blame their genetic makeup and believe they are the way they are, full of addictive behavioral problems because of their genetic makeup. We love this! We've got fat genes, addictive genes, alcohol genes, heroin genes, thief genes, and because of our "genetic makeup" we are not responsible. Christians blame the devil. Secular humanists don't believe in a devil because that would be too spooky, so they blame your genes. And if it's not your genes, it's your corduroys, or your khakis!

What has to happen to whip these behaviors? There are genetic issues, but I'm convinced God gave us the power to rule over our flesh. The war is not with our genetic makeup. A renewed mind will change your physical body. When you get your mind renewed, then you're not going to suck on cigarettes anymore. You can replace cigarettes, but it all comes back to one issue: *When my thinking changes, then I'll break the habit.*

At nineteen, I was in a drug rehabilitation center. I had quit smoking pot, snorting coke, and sticking needles in my arm. One day I asked myself, "Why am I doing this?" My thinking about cigarettes and drugs changed. I no longer needed them to feel good or to look good. I was really tired of yellow fingernails and green teeth! It's a bummer, because kissing a smoker is like kissing an ashtray! I was trying to find someone to kiss me, you know, so I needed to clean up.

When my thinking about cigarettes changed, I quit smoking in one day. No patches. No pills. No packs of gum.

So what's the key to breaking habits and having your unlimited life? *Capturing every thought and bringing it into obedience to Christ.* If you will train yourself to capture thoughts and bring them into agreement with God's Word, you can kick cigarettes or any other bad habit.

The stronghold is in your thinking, and when those thoughts from the world, from the tree of the knowledge of good and evil have a strong hold on you, that's the area that has to be renewed. Your unlimited life is not far away, it's a matter of capturing and replacing thoughts. The next chapter will teach you how this is not an impossible feat but a matter of basic daily steps.

Personal Application of Renewal Truths

1. I accept God's Word as the highest standard of truth in the following areas of my life: _____

    _____

    _____

    _____

2. To be created in God's image and likeness means:

    _____

    _____

    _____

3. The power and authority of Satan and his demonic spirits isn't the challenge we face today. It is:

    _____

    _____

4. Lies bring,_____

    but truth brings_____

    _____

5. The source of my thoughts, words, and actions is:

    _____

    _____

    _____

6. I am closing the door so the devil will have *no entrance* into my life to influence me or contaminate my thoughts by: _____

   _____

   _____

7. Our battles are won or lost in the arena of the:

   _____

   _____

   _____

   _____

8. I am bringing my thoughts into obedience to Christ by:

   _____

   _____

   _____

   _____

   _____

   _____

   _____

   _____

   _____

   _____

   _____

   _____

   _____

4

REPLACING NEGATIVE HABITS

While driving to church years ago, my son Caleb said, "Dad, they ought to let ten-year-olds drive." I said, "Boy, that would be a wild thing." He said, "At least twelve-year-olds. I can drive better than a lot of people I know." He was probably right!

Caleb was learning and growing, and inside of him was a desire to get bigger and better and do more. As adults, our desires may be buried under fears and failures, but there is still a desire to be like your Father. The Bible says we were predestined to be conformed to the image of Jesus Christ. There is a desire in all of us for continual growth and transformation. I want to change. I want to be like Jesus, who submitted to the will of the Father and even when they hung Him on a tree, He obeyed God.

The spirit of the natural man wants to argue and fight. I have counseled couples who were ready to divorce because of fighting and screaming over the color of towels in the bathroom. We've all heard the jokes of people arguing over which way the toilet paper is supposed to hang, rolled out or rolled in. Simple solution: Just get two rolls and do one each way!

Many people come to our church and I know we tell them the truth, but some don't come back because they don't want to hear it. They don't want to change their habits.

A habit is a thought or a way of thinking that causes us to function in the same routines all of our adult life. It is a repeated thought or behavior that becomes so automatic that it is difficult to stop. It can become an addiction, a custom or a tradition.

Most of our habits, whether good or bad, were picked up by watching the habits of those around us. If kids grow up where Mom and Dad take showers, comb their hair, and dress properly, most likely they will do the same thing.

The Bible says in Proverbs 22:6, *"Train up a child in the way he should go, and when he is old he will not depart from it."* When he is young, he may depart from it for a while, but he will come back to the teachings of his early childhood.

Time-Released Beliefs

Have you done things for a season in your life that were contrary to the habits of your parents, but then somewhere around thirty or thirty-five, you realized how much like your parents you had become? When children grow up, they won't depart from what they were taught. I call their habits "time-released beliefs."

Usually, when you start to do something that becomes a habit, it's not easy at first, but you do it repeatedly until it becomes easy. The first cigarette doesn't taste good, although you try to act cool. You turn green, cough, and vomit. But many people keep at it until it becomes a habit. Other people get in the habit of watching soap operas.

For more than thirty years, I've gone to a little restaurant in the Seattle area that makes good ribs. You can only go there about once every six months, because it takes that long to get the fat and cholesterol out of your system! You can tell they are good ribs because the floor is so greasy you just slide in there! So I slide in and get a pound of pork ribs -- the small ends that fall off the bone -- and some white bread!

Every time I go there, they've got a TV on and they're watching, "As My Stomach Turns," or some soap opera. Those guys love me. They say, "Praise the Lord, Pastor. It's been a long time since you've been here. How's the church doing? Has the Lord been good to you? Good to see you. You're going to have the usual? Small end? Praise the Lord!"

Now how can you be praising God, working in your business, and watching "All My Hopelessness," "The Terrible Hospital," and "As My Stomach Turns"? They know the characters on the shows as well as they know me. It's a habit. It's a stronghold.

Christians can have negative, worldly habits just like non-Christians. It's a way of thinking and acting that you repeat until it becomes a part of your life. Often times it has become such an integral part of our lives we will not even take note of it when we are reflecting on things we need to change.

You can develop habits with sex, money, food, and many other things. Habits are formed by repeated thoughts and actions. They have nothing to do with good or bad, right or wrong. If you think something and do it repeatedly, it will become a habit.

Your spirit, soul, and body are designed to grasp things and hang onto them. God's idea is that we get the Word of God in us, hang onto it, and not let it go. But if we pump the world into us, the same thing will happen.

God's plan was that He would fill Adam so full of the truth that he would hang onto it and live that truth forever. That was His plan for all mankind.

The "Process" of Breaking Habits

One great thing about being a born-again person is that you can break old habits. You can stop the process. You can turn the repeated thoughts and behavior around. You do not have to be stuck in your old ways any more. Your unlimited life doesn't have to be a dream but can become a reality.

How long does it take to turn negative habits around? I believe a minimum of forty days. God gave us a mark at forty. Moses was forty days on the mountain. Jesus was forty days in the wilderness. I believe it will take you forty days to get anything going, but even then, you can backslide in a hurry. Generally, it takes two or three years to make something a part of your life. Forty days will get you started. Then, after two or three years, it will become a part of your life.

Most people just want a touch to break a habit. You can get that too, but that's just step one. After you fall to the floor from the power of God, you've got to get up. Getting you on the floor is not hard, but it's what happens when you get up that we're focussed on in this book.

How Long Did You Practice That Bad Habit?

We spend years doing certain things, and then we want them changed overnight. We follow the devil twenty-seven years, come to God, and say, "Straighten me out, Lord." We spend years with bad eating habits and we want everything to be different in thirty days or less and that's just not real. A long-term follow-through is needed.

Most of our habits are picked up by watching the habits of those around us. We hear an accent and pretty soon we are talking like the people we are around. When I go overseas, I talk differently according to the country I am in. This is the reason we've got to be careful who we hang out with. Soon we'll smell like them, sound like them, and be like them.

RENEWAL TRUTH

I am a companion of those

who keep God's Word.

(Psalm 119:63)

If you are having a problem with finances, look at whom you are hanging out with. If you are having a problem with your health, look at whom you are hanging out with. If you have a problem with your temper, whom are you hanging out with?

REPLACING NEGATIVE HABITS WITH POSITIVE ONES

Habits are not so much stopped as they are *replaced*. It's not just a matter of stopping the negative; it's a matter of developing something positive to replace the negative.

Foolish parents say to their children, "Don't do that." Wise parents say, "Come over here and do this." When you say, "Don't do that," a child's immediate response is "Why?" They are instantly then drawn even more towards that which they are not allowed to do. Wise parents *replace* the thought and the action.

When a child is near breakable objects, instead of saying, "Don't touch that," say, "Look at this stuffed animal. Let's play with it." Replace what you don't want them to have with something they can have.

If I preach all day on what you shouldn't do, all you will do when you go out of church is think about everything you shouldn't do. This is why we preach more on righteousness, encouraging you towards it rather than on sin.

RENEWAL TRUTH
I am the righteousness of God
in Christ Jesus.
(2 Corinthians 5:21)

Yelling at your wife constantly is a bad habit, in order to stop you must replace the way in which you communicate by using a nicer tone. Rather than stopping the negative cold, we want to replace it. You can replace overeating with, "I'm going to get healthy"; anger with, "I'm going to start being kind"; and cursing with, "I'm going to speak words of grace." If you focus on what you are stopping, you will probably never stop it.

A wise coach doesn't say to his player, "Stop swinging the bat that way." Instead he says, "Swing the bat at this level." Get the person focused on what you want, not on what you don't want.

Philippians 4:8 says:

Finally, brethren, whatever things are true, whatever things are noble, whatever things are just, whatever things are pure, whatever things are lovely, whatever things are of good report, if there is any virtue and if there is anything praiseworthy - meditate on these things.

Notice, it doesn't state all the things that you are not supposed to think about. It lists the things you are to focus on. Breaking a habit is not stopping something as much as it is starting something.

KEYS TO BREAKING OLD HABITS AND BUILDING NEW ONES

Some of the keys to breaking old habits and building new ones are:

Key #1: Desire something different.

Desire sparks change. I desire windows that are not yellow from smoke and fingers and teeth that are not stained. I desire lungs that are not black. When you desire something you didn't desire before, you are ready to break an old habit and start a new one. If there is no desire, nothing is going to happen.

Psalm 37:4 says:

Delight yourself also in the Lord, and He shall give you the desires of your heart.

When you desire to be healthy, you will begin to change your eating and exercise habits. As long as there is no desire for a long life of health and fitness, you can buy the books, tapes, equipment, programs, and vitamins, but there will be no change. The beginning of your change is the desire to change.

Key #2: Begin to picture yourself with that new thought, action, and lifestyle.

The hardest thing for me to do when I became a Christian was to see myself never using drugs, never drinking alcohol, and never having to go to a chemical substance for some kind of feeling. I was a Christian and hadn't used drugs for almost a year before I could really see myself making that change.

Now the difference between me and most of the people around me at that time is, they weren't working on a new picture, so they lived drug-free for a year and then went right back to it. What about the person who loses fifty pounds and then gains sixty? They never get a new picture. They may change for a season, but they never get a new picture of themselves in their mind.

For almost a year I worked on a new perspective of myself: "I'll never smoke another cigarette; I'll never smoke another joint; I'll never snort another line of coke; I'll never stick another needle in my arm. I will be free from that." This means, "I'll find my satisfaction from other sources. I will build new and better relationships."

Most people never get to the place where they get a "new picture" of themselves. Though they may change for a season, without a new picture, they go right back to their old habits.

RENEWAL TRUTH

I am framing my life with what God says about me
in His Word. He says He has a future and a hope for me,
filled with peace and free of evil.
(Hebrews 11:3; Jeremiah 29:11)

It's like the guy with a temper. He tries to convince himself that he is not going to shout, yell, or scream. He fully intends to stay cool and calm and trains himself to hide all emotion and passion within. He eventually has an emotional breakdown or suffers depression because he didn't get a new picture of himself. He held his feelings inside. What he should have done was to say, "I'm a kind, thoughtful person. I see myself communicating, not yelling. I see myself listening and understanding, not angrily controlling. I see myself building intimacy in relationships, not pushing others away." This new picture of himself could have enabled him to walk free of anger rather than to keep it bottled up inside.

For lifestyle issues, we are talking about months of consistency changing the way we think and months of looking at the "new you."

Out of nearly 3,000 young people who entered the drug rehab program, I was one of the few who completed it. Today I can count less than a dozen of those people who stayed clean. The others didn't change their picture of themselves. Changing the picture of your life is as simple as viewing a new tomorrow. Your unlimited life is on the other side of the eraser and new canvas.

Joshua 1:8 is the Scripture for Key #2:

This Book of the Law shall not depart from your mouth, but you shall meditate in it day and night, that you may observe to do according to all that is written in it. For then you will make your way prosperous, and then you will have good success.

Key #3: Talk about the way you want to be, not the way you are.

Start communicating in a new way. Instead of saying things like, "It makes me so mad," say, "I am beginning to understand another point of view." You have to speak new words before you will get new feelings. Nothing "makes" you anything. You have the power to choose how you feel. You have to say things like, "I used to live for my next meal, but now food isn't that important to me." Your desire may be that you are desiring something to eat, but your words are, "You know, food isn't that important to me anymore."

Jesus said:

For assuredly, I say to you, whoever says to this mountain, "Be removed and be cast into the sea," and does not doubt in his heart, but believes that those things he says will be done, he will have whatever he says.

Mark 11:23

What have you been saying? "I can't believe how hard it is. This diet is killing me." If that's not what you want, don't say it. "I've been trying to quit smoking, but I'm telling you, every time I look around, somebody is lighting up, and it is driving me crazy." If that's not what you want, don't say it. What you need to say is, "To quit smoking is easy." You may not feel that way. But you say, "To quit smoking is no big deal. I'll whip it easily." *Start speaking what you desire to achieve and you will have success.*

RENEWAL TRUTH
Like the example God gave me,
I will call those things which do not exist as though they
did. They will manifest because God cannot lie.
He will make good on all of His promises.
(Romans 4:17; Numbers 23:19)

You can say, "Losing weight is easy for me, because my metabolism is right. I am designed to lose weight and I can take it off!" In their struggle to lose weight, some people lay hands on the scale and believe for the demons to be cast out of the scale! Others say, "I didn't eat anything for three months and I gained two pounds." Or, "Everything I eat goes right on my belly!" We're not talking about just stopping something. We are talking about replacing the negative with something new and different. If you make a decision to turn the power to remain negative around into the power to be positive, your entire life will change.

Key #4: Practice thinking and doing the new thing every

day.

Repetition makes something a part of you. Anything you want to be good at, you have to practice. "Wishing" something were different won't bring the change. You have to practice. If you want to play golf and be good at it, you have to practice. If you want to play baseball and be good at it, you have to practice. Many people want the change, but they don't want the practice that goes with it.

Practice your new thoughts every day. Spend five or ten minutes a day seeing yourself as a new person. Say it out loud to yourself: "I am that new person. I am a kind, gentle, and patient person." Make your new thoughts, confessions, and actions a normal part of your daily behavior. If you only work on it on Sundays when you go to church, then not much is going to change. Six days of doing your old thing and one day of trying something new won't make much difference. James 1:25 says, "You will be blessed in what you do." The more you practice the "new you," the more change will come, the more blessings will come, and the more renewal will come.

Many times it's helpful to get two or three friends to interact with you as you practice so you can be a help and support to each other. If you hang around people who are doing what you are doing, they will be an encouragement to you and you will also be an encouragement to them.

Key #5: You have to get to the place where the new thing is "normal" in your mind.

If it never gets to the place where it is normal, then you won't change. It's normal for me to wake up early and pray, but it's abnormal for me to exclaim to Wendy, "Wow! I'm telling you, today I was in the Holy Ghost!" That's not the real me. It's an aberration because it's not normal. Waking up early and seeking God in the morning is normal to me. Giving is normal to me. It's part of my lifestyle. I do it all the time, like breathing. Patience and kindness are normal to me. It's normal for me to be a leader and set the pace for others to follow. You have to get your routine into your mind until you say, "That's the way I am."

RENEWAL TRUTH

As I think in my heart, so am I.
I see myself victorious in Christ Jesus
in achieving the destiny God has set before me.
(Proverbs 23:7; 1 Corinthians 15:57)

Using athletes as an example, when you go to the plate and hit a home run and then you're excitedly asking everyone around you if they saw it, then we know that's not normal for you. That was unusual for you. When you do something good and someone goes, "Wow! You've really changed," you respond, "That's just the way I am." "I remember before, you'd have been throwing a fit right now, slamming the door, and kicking the cat." "But this is the way I am. It's normal to me now." You have to make it part of you so that it's no longer something that you are hoping for.

Key #6: When you slip back (or backslide), get up and go on without condemnation.

When you fail, fall, stumble, or go back on your old routine, acknowledge the mistake then continue on from where you left off. Don't go all the way back to the beginning, because you've made a lot of progress. Just get up and go on, free of condemnation.

The devil will always, without fail, try and bring condemnation and guilt on you. He will try and convince you that you are a failure, haven't changed at all, and are really still the same person. His lies will make you feel like it is pointless to try and change, saying, "Look at you. You talk about being patient and kind. Now you've gone off and put your fist through the wall again." Patch it up, or hang a picture over the hole, and get back to your routine of, "I'm a kind, gentle, and patient person." One step back doesn't mean you've lost it all, so don't let the devil condemn you.

RENEWAL TRUTH

I will not receive condemnation,
because I no longer walk according to the flesh.
I am a child of God, and I am led by His Spirit.
(Romans 8:1,14)

Many people mess up on their way to their improved self. They may be on a new eating program and they've lost five pounds. They feel good about themselves. Then one day they eat a bag of Cheetos and in their mind they convince themselves it's over, they blew it! All is not lost. Pick up from where you left off and keep right on going, recognizing that a few missteps are a normal part of the process. That doesn't mean you should excuse it to the point you take a step back every day, but if it happens, don't let it be the end of your journey. Pick up and press on, acknowledge that it is not you anymore. Tell yourself that you are not going to make that mistake again and then move on.

If you carry guilt and condemnation, you are preparing to repeat that behavior again. But when you really decide to move on, let it go and go on about your business. Walk the renewal process free of guilt but full of focused determination.

Key #7: Be alert to past weaknesses that may resurface.

Usually what happens is, once you've had some success, you relax and the tendency is to slip back into the old behaviors again. Right after David had won a great victory for Israel, instead of going out with his troops as he should have done, he stayed home and rose from bed in the middle of the day. Looking from the roof of his house, he spied a married woman, Bathsheba, as she was bathing on a nearby rooftop.

As a result of his affair with Bathsheba and his plot to kill her husband, which was carried out, he entered into one of the greatest seasons of pain and defeat of his life. This all took place right after one of his greatest victories. (See 2 Samuel, chapter 11.)

As you make progress, don't allow yourself to slip back into some of your old habits or routines. This is where people get into the cycle of up and down. Habits are kind of like ruts in a road. It's easy to slip into the ruts, but it's harder to get out of them.

To stay out of them takes a conscious effort, but to get into them takes little or no effort.

When I was a kid, we used to ride motorcycles on a military reservation. Before it was a military reservation, there were many homes, orchards, and farms on the property. There were many old roads, driveways, and cart-ways that had grown over with weeds, but we knew that we could still get through on our horses and motorcycles. We could reopen old roads much easier than we could build new ones.

In your attitudes and mind-sets, you will reopen old roads much easier than building new ones. So be alert to keep from slipping into some of the old routines again.

Remember, we talked briefly about "time-released beliefs," where attitudes surface that you had no idea were a part of you, because as a young person they weren't a part of your lifestyle.

But when you hit thirty-five, suddenly you start acting like your mom. When you hit forty, you start talking about things that you picked up from your parents. At fifty, you start saying things that you had never thought before. Suddenly, you realize that you are talking like people in your past. That's what I call "time-released beliefs."

We have a video where I am giving Caleb a bath the day he was born. A few minutes after his birth in our home, I had him in the sink. I watched this video and realized I was talking just like my dad. I never talked like that before, but I'd never been a dad before. So at the moment of my son's birth, a time-released belief went off in me. I picked up thoughts and behaviors and words that I'd heard from my father and began to repeat them to my son. That caused me to realize I'd better plug in here be-cause I would probably discipline him the way I was disciplined without even thinking about it. I would probably do things with him the way things were done with me without even thinking about it. There are some great things that I got from my dad, but I needed to be aware of time-released beliefs.

If you are in your twenties or thirties, age is not a great con-cern to you yet. But when you are sixty, your attitude about age will surface and you'll start saying and doing things that you never thought were inside of you. That's why we need to be extremely intentional about programming ourselves to say what God says about us starting now, at whatever age you are.

Everyone we're around is checking out at seventy or eighty. They are not planning to live beyond seventy or eighty. They're middle-aged at forty and are preparing to die at sixty. If they make it to seventy or eighty, they're talking about how they re-ally had a good life. If you're going to go beyond that, you have generations of thoughts, words, and attitudes to break.

Fred Price from Crenshaw Christian Center in Los Angeles taught me years ago that God gave me 120 years. Genesis 6:3 says, *"The years of man are 120."* So I began to program myself that I was going to live until 120. I'm not going to be middle-aged at forty or fifty. At sixty, I will celebrate middle age. You have to program it into your mind and come against those time-released beliefs.

When some people hit forty, they start to confess and tell others that they are over the hill. No! I'm still on my way up. That's why, in my fifties, I'm doing things I've never done when

73

I was twenty. Things I've never done before, stretching myself physically, mentally, and spiritually beyond where I've ever been before. I'm still on my way up! When I'm sixty I will say, "Now I'm at the top of the hill." Then I can start charging into the last half of my life. It's a whole new mind-set. You have to fight the old belief and most people don't have the guts to fight it. The majority of people repeat the cycle of life that has been modeled for them and inevitably do what they were raised to do. We are not the average. We are fighting for our unlimited life.

We may not get the full benefits of what we are committed to in the areas of change and renewal, but we can pass something on to the next generation so they can go beyond us. If we hand them the ability to get out of the rut, out of the routine, and not get stuck in the old ways, then we've done them a great service. We're not just living for ourselves. We're living for the next generations. We're not just doing this for what we get on this earth, but for what we can give to the generations that follow.

Years ago T. L. Osborn said to me, "I may not make 120, but if I reach for it, maybe somebody following me will make it. If I don't reach for it, they probably won't reach for it either." Someone has to start the process and break the norm, then pass it on. We are those people. We will believe for more.

Personal Application of Renewal Truths

1. Identify negative habits in your own life that you want to replace with positive habits:

Negative Habit   Positive Replacement

_____   _____

_____   _____

_____   _____

_____   _____

_____   _____

_____   _____

_____   _____

2. Instead of focusing on negative habits, I will focus on things that are (see Philippians 4:8):

a. _____

b. _____

c. _____

d. _____

e. _____

f. _____

g. _____

h. _____

3. I am speaking what I desire to achieve, which is:

_____

_____

_____

_____

_____

_____

_____

4. Daily practicing new thoughts about myself will:

_____

_____

_____

_____

_____

_____

_____

_____

_____

_____

_____

_____

_____

_____

5

TRUTH BRINGS LIGHT

Be sober, be vigilant; because your adversary the devil walks about like a roaring lion, seeking whom he may devour.

1 Peter 5:8

Satan is the source of all evil, but his power is limited. He can't do anything he wants, nor can he touch just anybody he wants to touch. He is seeking whom he may devour. That tells us that he can only devour the lives of those who will allow him to do so.

We must be sober, self-controlled, vigilant, and watchful because Satan is constantly on the prowl, seeking someone to devour. 1 Peter 5:9 says, ***"Resist him, steadfast in the faith, knowing..."*** In other words, what you know is a major part of resisting the devil. Resisting him in the faith means that you can resist him with the Word because faith comes by hearing, and hearing by the Word of God (Romans 10:17). If you don't know the Word, you can't resist the devil, remaining steadfast in the faith.

There is no resistance to the devil available from secular magazines, newspapers, or even motivational speakers. We must have truth (God's Word) working in us and flowing out of us to resist the devil.

A bank teller is trained to recognize counterfeit money, not by handling the counterfeit, but by handling the "real" stuff! We don't need to spend time studying cults to recognize them. If we know the Word, we will be able to recognize the devil's lies in whatever form they come.

I did not teach my children how to smoke pot so they would recognize it. I tried to teach them how to live righteously and how to use sound judgment. As a result, they can discern and understand things that are unrighteous. *If you are full of the Word, you will understand anything that is not of the Word.*

Years ago I had a friend who taught comparative religions in churches and did seminars on the occult. He came to a point where he went totally bonkers. He was depressed and discouraged. One day I asked him what was going on and why the downturned countenance? He said, "I have spent so much time talking about what is wrong, it has destroyed my faith. I am not going to do any more seminars. I am doing nothing but reading the Word, getting my relationship back with God, and plugging in to the truth." Truth will keep you free. If you talk about lies long enough, they will bring you into bondage.

Jesus said in John 10:10 that Satan comes to steal, kill, and destroy. But what has to happen before he can do that and get away with it? He has to get us to believe a lie. He has to steal truth from us. If Satan can get you to believe a lie about your spouse, he can destroy your marriage. One such lie is, "He [or she] is not going to change, and you deserve to be happy. Leave him [or her] and get on with your life."

You start thinking, "That's right." Then you have to spiritualize a lie: "Doesn't God want me to be happy? If God wants me to be happy, then He must want me to leave my husband [or wife] because the only way I can be happy is to get away from him [her]." Now a lie, made to sound Christ-like, is running your life and is originated, by the devil, in deceit.

How often in life do we seek to find a co-signer for a lie, so you find a friend and say, "I've been thinking about leaving my husband because the Lord wants me to be happy." The friend is sober and vigilant, so she says, "Sister, you are way off base. God called you to a lifetime commitment. God is going to bless your marriage and your faithfulness. He is going to change your marriage. Scripture says you can sanctify your husband. Let's believe and pray the Word and turn this thing around."

You are looking for someone to co-sign your lie, and your friend keeps bringing you the truth, so you go to another friend. "I think God wants me to leave my husband. Doesn't God want me to be happy?" You've found someone who has the same lie working in them. She has a poor relationship, too. So this person says, "I think you are right. There is no condemnation in Christ, and God has not called us to bondage. I think you'd better leave that chump. You will probably be better off without him." Now you've got a co-signer. The two of you agree and you start acting on the lie.

The same thing happens when you decide you are not going to tithe or you are not going to be committed to a church. Most of the time people do not leave a church by themselves. They leave in groups because they don't have the guts to act on a lie by themselves. They have to find a co-signer to act on their lie. Sometimes people leave their church so they can get rid of their spouse. Or, they leave their church so they can stop serving and giving. Be alert to people who are looking for a co-signer for their lie. Be the first friend in this illustration, a person who, regardless of the situation at hand, will stand firm on the ways of God and the truth of His Word.

RENEWAL TRUTH

If the truth sets you free,

then lies will bring you into bondage.

(John 8:31-32)

How Jesus Handled the Devil's Lies

In Matthew 4, Jesus gives us an example of how to handle the devil's lies and deceptions.

> *Then Jesus was led up by the Spirit into the wilderness to be tempted by the devil. And when He had fasted forty days and forty nights, afterward He was hungry. Now when the tempter came to Him, he said, "If You are the Son of God, command that these stones become bread."*
>
> Matthew 4:1-3

This lie questions Jesus' identity: ***"If You are the Son of God."*** The voice of God had already revealed Jesus' identity: ***"This is My beloved Son, in whom I am well pleased"*** (Matthew 3:17). Satan's question was to the voice of God and to the Word of God. What happens when you get thoughts, such as:

• "If I was healed, it seems like I'd feel better."

- "If God wanted to prosper my life, it seems like I'd have more money."
- "If the Word was true, it seems like things would be different."

Satan does the same thing to you that he did to Jesus. "If you are the Son of God, do something to prove it." He was planting a seed of doubt and unbelief by asking Jesus to prove His identity.

Remember, Genesis 3:1 said, ***"The serpent was more cunning than any beast of the field."*** The issue here with Jesus' confrontation by the devil isn't about power; it's about his ability to lie and deceive.

Satan has been stripped of his authority, but he has some power. It is his subtleties that we have to deal with. You can wipe out his power with the name of Jesus the same day you are saved! That doesn't mean you are smart enough to keep from being tricked, deceived, or lied to, which is the issue. We are so worried about having power over the devil that we fail to realize that is not the problem. We've got power over the devil, but if he lies to us and we are dull in our thinking and hearing, he is able to succeed in deceiving us.

Satan said to Jesus, ***If You are the Son of God, command that these stones become bread*** (Matthew 4:3). After forty days of fasting, it was natural for Jesus to want some bread. Wouldn't it have been a natural response for Him to say, "I have the right to make some bread. I am God and I am hungry"? Satan always sets you up in a position where it would seem okay to go ahead and flow with his lie. That's what happens when people compromise. "Don't I have the right to be happy?" Well, of course you do! "To be happy I am going to have to leave my spouse," or, "I am going to have to have sex before I am married," or, "I can't tithe this month." Satan sets us up to compromise Scripture and to go against the Word of God.

One argument of the secular world is, "Are you telling me that a woman who has been raped and becomes pregnant, should she bear the burden and carry the pain all of her life and make a child suffer for that terrible crime?" "No, I wouldn't tell you that. I guess you'd better go ahead and kill the baby." See, it seems logical. How could we be so terrible as to put the woman through that?

We missed the whole point. How can we, as a society, get to the place where we kill our kids? Let's get back to reality instead of considering what seems and feels and sounds right. When we start reasoning with the devil, we get caught up in deception.

The devil says to Jesus, "If You are the Son of God, make bread." That sounds good. What is wrong with making bread after fasting for forty days and forty nights? Obviously, Jesus whipped the devil so why would He need to make bread? Is it only to prove that He is the Son of God? Why would He have to prove it? Because we don't believe what God said: *"This is My beloved Son."* It all goes back to *questioning the Word.* Anytime you are lied to by the devil, in the end, it gets back to questioning the Word.

Jesus said, *"It is written, 'Man shall not live by bread alone, but by every word that proceeds from the mouth of God'"*

(Matthew 4:4). What Word came from God? *"This is My beloved Son, in whom I am well pleased"* (Matthew 3:17). Jesus responded to Satan with the Word. We must have an understanding of the Word to keep ourselves free from Satan's lies. If you don't know the Word, you are susceptible to lies.

RENEWAL TRUTH

I am diligent to present myself approved unto God,

a worker who needs not to be ashamed,

rightly dividing the word of truth.

(2 Timothy 2:15)

How can someone who goes to church all their life be lied to and ripped off by the devil? People who have grown up in the church, faithful church members, deacons, and ushers, end up in adultery, fornication, poverty, disease, cancer, heart attacks, their kids pregnant, and their kids divorced. How can these things happen to good Christian people? Although they went to church all their life, *they didn't get the Word.* They got three poems and a magazine article. They got a social gospel by a robe-ridden preacher who was trying to keep his job and do his best. They got a denominational message that was rooted in tradition and religion, but they didn't get the Word. If there is no Word, you have nothing to live on because man lives by every Word from God.

People need to be fed the Word of God, not philosophy, denominational doctrine, or a social gospel. People need the Word in them. If you don't get the Word, you are open prey to the lies of the devil. Without receiving the Word and diligently applying it to your life, you are a direct target for the lies of Satan.

Some people choose a church because they feel loved there. I've got news for you: Love isn't going to save you from the lies of the devil. People are getting ripped off, going through divorce, and they are literally going through hell, while they sit in "nice" churches. Some come to Christian Faith Center and think we are too intense. We are serious. There is a war going on, and if you don't get the Word in you, you are not going to make it. We have fun but we also recognize the battle for mankind. I recognize that the devil wants your mind; I am committed to fight with you to get it back.

Some people opt for a "nice" environment where they will end up with their kids out in the world, but they feel good about the "niceness." That is a lie and a trick of the devil. We're not about "feeling nice." We are about making sure we have what it takes to live, and it takes a daily dose of God's Word.

RENEWAL TRUTH

Although grass withers and flowers fade,
the Word of God stands forever.
(Isaiah 40:8)

Jesus responded to the devil with clarity and boldness, stating that He didn't have to react by making bread, because He had the Word. Jesus did not buy into the temptation for food to prove who He was.

Then the devil took Him up into the holy city, set Him on the pinnacle of the temple, and said to Him, "If You are the Son of God, throw Yourself down. For it is written...."

Matthew 4:5-6

The devil throws in a Scripture: *"He shall give His angels charge over you,"* and, *"In their hands they shall bear you up, lest you dash your foot against a stone"* (v. 6).

Satan perverts Scripture, and many people who don't seek wise counsel will believe it. Through perverting Scripture, he will make you feel justified to do the very thing that will destroy your life. Many people have quoted Scripture to me and then went off into sin they claimed was supported by Scripture.

Case in point: Satan tempts you with another woman - "You have the right to be happy. This woman would love you, care for you, and be a good wife. You need to lose your present wife and go get a new one." If you don't respond, Satan will bring Scripture: "Scripture says the woman is supposed to submit to the man. Your wife is not submitting to you, so you have a right to leave her. Paul said in 1 Corinthians 7, "If she departs, let her depart." Now you have Scripture going around in your head to get you to sin.

People excuse and rationalize with Scripture. Jesus says, "No, I am not going to respond to you, Satan. I don't need bread to know who I am. I've got the Word of God."

Years ago I had a friend who traveled with me to Europe several times. He had a call of God on his life and was a great minister. He got in his head the crazy idea about leaving the church. He said he didn't need the church anymore; God was calling him elsewhere now. He quoted Scripture to me, put together a very compelling argument, and even convinced some of our friends. A month later he was totally gone — drinking, smoking weed, and he left his wife and children. His life is nowhere near the place God wanted it to be. He sold himself short by believing the lies and not capturing every thought that was contrary to the Word. The saddest part is — *he got there by quoting Scripture.*

I tried to counsel him telling him that's not what Scripture says. If you want to believe a lie, you can find a Scripture to back you up. This is where wise counsel and a multitude of counselors come in.

Jesus responded to Satan's lie, *"It is written again, 'You shall not tempt the Lord your God'"* (v. 7). Then Satan tried another temptation for glory, power, and position. *"Again, the devil took Him up on an exceedingly high mountain, showed Him all the kingdoms of the world and their glory. And he said to Him, "All these things I will give You if You will fall down and worship me"* (v. 8-9).

Satan had the power to give it to Jesus because it had been given to him from Adam. Jesus responded, *"Away with you, Satan! For it is written, "You shall worship the Lord your God, and Him only you shall serve"* (v. 10).

If you have a well-balanced perspective of Scripture, no matter what lie comes against you, you won't be tricked or deceived. Even Jesus, the Son of God, did not respond with what He thought at the moment. He responded with the logos -- the written Word of God. Jesus never said, "Well, I just don't feel good about this,

Mr. Devil." He responded with, "It is written," followed by an exact quote of Scripture that was appropriate for each situation.

Major ministries that have fallen in the last few years weren't teaching the Word. They were emotional and promotional, great salesmen and media personalities, but they weren't Word based, standing on the Word for every challange.

When you are not strong with, "It is written," your life will not have long-term success. It is worth it to be a Word person. In the longevity of your life, you will find greater levels of happiness, societal success, family blessings, and all good things if you stay committed to the Word.

RENEWAL TRUTH

Your Word is forever settled in heaven, Lord.
It is a lamp to my feet and a light to my path.
(Psalm 119:89,105)

How are we to overcome the lies that bind? With the truth that frees, which is God's Word. If you will stay focused on the Word, you will have what it takes to say, "It is written," and not be tricked by the devil.

Personal Application of Renewal Truths

1. To resist the devil, I must know God's Word. My knowledge of God's Word is growing by:

   _____

   _____

   _____

   _____

2. Satan's lies are exposed by:

   _____

   _____

   _____

   _____

3. Jesus gave me a "model" for dealing with Satan's lies. He handled the devil's lies by (see Matthew 4:1-11):

   _____

   _____

   _____

4. Does Satan's effectiveness come through power or through deception? Explain: _____

   _____

   _____

   _____

5. Satan has been stripped of authority. As a child of God, I can wipe out his power with the name of _____ .

6

THE ANOINTING
OF THE HOLY SPIRIT

*But you have an anointing from the Holy One, and you
know all things.*

1 John 2:20

As a young Christian, I did not understand this verse. There
were many times when I knew things, yet I'd convince myself I
must be wrong because I would think that I am *too young*, I can't
go against what society is telling me or what the preacher on the
TV is preaching - I'm too new in my Christianity. As time went
by, I found out that I was right. I knew something, either about an
individual, about a ministry, or about something going on. Now
that I look back, I realize the Holy Spirit anoints us to know.

In every area of life, we can trust God for an anointing to cor-
respond with what He has called us to do. You can't disregard
study or discipline, but you will have an anointing to know what
you need to know to function in your life.

I trust God for the anointing to know how to be a husband,
a father, and a pastor. 1 John 2 says: ***But the anointing which
you have received from Him abides in you.*** This is true for all
believers. The anointing doesn't come and go, it *abides*.

Now, one of the things that we have taught in our

cruise-a-matic, charismatic world, is the Holy Spirit comes upon us, does His thing, leaves, and we go back out to the real world. We have a mentality that says we go into the anointing and then we come out of it. Christian songs often portray the Holy Spirit as a fire that comes, then leaves or as a ghost that swoops down, then rushes back out. I am just as anointed at 7:00AM Monday morning as I was at 11:00AM on Sunday. The anointing abides in me.

If my daughter comes in at 8:00AM on Friday night and exclaims that she has a problem that is a major issue, I need the anointing of truth to help lead and guide her. I can't say, "Tasha, let's just wait, and see if the Holy Spirit anoints us tonight."

We need to get out of the mentality of something happening if the Holy Spirit shows up. Stop thinking: "Here He comes, when we all get to heaven, in a little while, or when the revival hits..." We need to get out of waiting for something from heaven and start recognizing the Holy Spirit has been poured out upon all flesh. He abides in us, and now as we are renewing our minds, we know truth and that truth is what is setting people free.

RENEWAL TRUTH

I shall decree what should be - in line with God's Word,
which is His will - and it shall be established.
(Job 22:28 KJV)

The anointing lives and abides in us. We are not always sensitive to it or aware of it, but it is always there. He will never leave us or forsake us. Let me throw this one in for free: Most of the time what we consider the anointing in a service is simply getting our faith turned on and getting excited about what God can do. It is more of an emotional thing in our lives than a change in the spirit world, not that the Holy Ghost doesn't come in and do unique things at times. But the reality is - the Holy Spirit is always with us! He never leaves and He doesn't only come to the church services where we ask Him to join us.

1 John 2:27 goes on: *And you do not need that anyone teach you* [this means that you know what is right and how the Holy Spirit is leading, because you have an anointing that abides in you]; *but as the same anointing teaches you concerning all things, and is true, and is not a lie, and just as it has taught you, you will abide in Him.*

The Holy Spirit leads us into all truth, not into lies. What about the preacher that says it is not mandatory that you pray in tongues. He explains that you just need to do what he tells you to do. He will tell you what is right; he will explain the necessary doctrines to live by. Follow those denominational practices and traditions and you will live just fine.

In such cases, we have done away with the need for a personal relationship with Jesus Christ and we have just become another religious group. We have to be careful that we do not start relying on 24-hour-a-day Christian television to have other people answer all of our questions. If Christian television, your pastor, your home group leader, your mentor, and everybody else could answer every question, then why would you need the Holy Spirit? Each of us needs a personal relationship with God, and each one of us must learn to listen to the Holy Spirit.

Usually when you ask other people a question, you already know the answer. You are just trying to find someone to confirm what you believe, or you are looking for a way out of what you know you are supposed to do. Because the anointing abides in you, you know the truth.

How come more people aren't sensitive to the Spirit? Their minds aren't renewed to the Word, so they get confused by their many goofy thoughts. If you could put the average person's brain on a video screen, it would scare you! You would have Halloween right in front of your face because the average person is so caught up in the thoughts and attitudes of the world that, though they love God, they have not been transformed to believe, think, and act like God believes, thinks, and acts.

RENEWAL TRUTH

I am being transformed continually by the renewing
of my mind with God's Word, that I may know the good,
acceptable, and perfect will of God.

(Romans 12:2)

I believe to love God with all your heart, soul, and mind means to have your soul plugged in, loving God with your mind, emotions, and will. I want you to really understand that when I say heart and soul I mean "with all your mind." That means you are going to have to change every thought that is contrary to loving God.

In raising my children, if they had attitudes that did not reveal a love for God, I had to help them get plugged into the

Word and get their thoughts changed. It is natural for us to have negative attitudes. We can all be immature in regards to our spiritual growth. The world and the flesh are negative. So if you do not love God with all your heart, soul, and mind, then you are going to have all kinds of problems. You won't be able to flow in the anointing, which will lead you into all truth. Your mind is set on lies, compromises, fears, worries, and negative things so what you are feeling inside isn't registering because your mind isn't sensitive to it.

When people listen to a song, some people only hear the lyrics, while others hear the instruments and the melodies, depending on the habits of listening. A piano tuner has his ear tuned to the right tone and he can hear a variation in tone that you or I might not hear. He plays the notes and quickly knows which white keys and black keys are out of pitch; meanwhile we would most likely think it sounded perfect. The difference is — his ear is trained.

My friend Terry Tarsiuk and I were listening to a CD in my car one day. He said, "Man, I love the instrumental," and started naming weird instruments I'd never even heard of. I replied, "I didn't hear any of that, but wow did you catch that drum line?" While I am sensitive to drums because that is what I play, he is sensitive to the other instruments because that is what he is into. Whatever you train your ear to hear, that is what you will hear.

While sitting in a room with a group of people, suddenly a mother jumps to her feet and rushes to find her baby because she hears her baby's cry. You may be sitting there and didn't hear a sound. Her ear is tuned to her child. Most mothers can even determine the difference in the "kind" of cry, whether it's a "hungry" cry, a "change me" cry, or a "hold me" cry.

The same thing happens in the Christian walk. When your mind is renewed to the truth, your ear is dialed to the anointing because the anointing leads you into all truth. Your ear is tuned to truth because you have renewed your mind to truth. As the anointing begins to flow, you know what God is doing and you know His will. But if your brain is like scrambled eggs, void of the anointing, you are confused, don't understand, and are scared, you will talk like an average person and live below God's ultimate desire for your life.

John said, *"Beloved, I pray that you may prosper in all things and be in health, just as your soul prospers"* (3 John 2). A "prosperous soul" is one that testifies of the truth that is in them and causes them to walk in truth.

For I rejoiced greatly when brethren came and testified of the truth that is in you, just as you walk in the truth. I have no greater joy than to hear that my children walk in truth.

3 John 1:3-4

This person abides in the truth of God's Word, and the Spirit of truth leads and guides them into all truth because they are sensitive to it.

The anointing that leads and guides them into all truth flows freely so they are prospering in their soul. They are plugged into the truth, both through the Word and through the anointing. Now they have health and prosperity in every area of life. It works. But, if you reject truth and don't have time for truth, the Spirit of truth can't work and the anointing can't flow. Everything gets jammed up, and you will have problems in your life. The voice of the Holy Spirit is not an audible voice, you won't be able to learn the actual timbre as you would a human's voice. It is by training your spirit to be sensitive to His guidance that you will find spiritual answers. Your soul prospers, you lead in your daily life, and you succeed in hardships depending on the level of truth that is operating in your life.

PAUL PRAYS TRUTH UPON THE CHURCH AT EPHESUS

In Ephesians 1, Paul is praying for the church at Ephesus. What is good for the church at Ephesus is good for us. He says:

Therefore I also, after I heard of your faith in the Lord Jesus and your love for all the saints, do not cease to give thanks for you, making mention of you in my prayers: that the God of our Lord Jesus Christ, the Father of glory, may give to you the spirit of wisdom and revelation in the knowledge of Him.

Ephesians 1:15-17

"The spirit of wisdom and revelation in the knowledge of God" refers to the Spirit of truth. The Spirit of truth brings wisdom (how to apply the truth) and revelation (a revealing of the truth) of the knowledge of God. Paul is praying that the work of the Holy Spirit will happen in this young church's life because he knows that their success, victory, and prosperity as Christians are dependent upon their walk in truth. It is not dependent on how many miracles they have seen.

RENEWAL TRUTH

Because God's power (His Spirit) is at work in me,
He is able to do exceedingly abundantly
above all that I could ever ask or think.
(Ephesians 3:20)

Wisdom is to know truth and to know how to apply it. How do we know when a person is wise? They do things that work and that bring good results.

A woman may know about proper relationships with men and about guarding and protecting her life, but that doesn't mean she is a wise woman. But, when a woman doesn't get involved with carnal men, or become trapped in her emotions and desires for improper relationships, and doesn't find herself being used and abused by men of the world, then we would say, "This is a wise woman." It is in her application of truth that we see wisdom.

Praying for Others

How can we pray for people in our churches and families to help them be the people God wants them to be? To help them find success in their lives?

In verse 17 of Ephesians, chapter 1, when Paul speaks of the Spirit of wisdom, he is speaking of the *Spirit of God* - not some angelic spirit, a human spirit, or a demonic spirit. It is the Spirit of God who brings wisdom and revelation in the knowledge of God.

When we pray for people, we pray that they will be healed. We pray that people will prosper. We pray that they will have success in life. But notice, when Paul prays for them, he prays that they will *know the right things*. That is the key for them to be healed, prospered, and to have success in life. When John prays for them in 3 John 2, he prays that they will prosper, *even as their soul prospers,* because he knows that is the key to their success in life.

Far too often, we pray for a change of the symptoms rather than a change of the root cause of the symptoms. We want the body healed, but we fail to go after the thing that caused the sickness in the first place. Remember back to the beginning of this book, the issue is the root and not the fruit. We want the checking account to be prosperous, but we fail to identify what made us poor in the first place. If we go after the spirit of wisdom and revelation in the knowledge of God, then healing, prosperity, and success will come. Why? Because now we are abiding in the anointing and the anointing is leading and guiding us into all truth. And when you know the truth, you will prosper in all things.

RENEWAL TRUTH

Because I abide in Jesus and His Word abides in me,

whatever I ask in line with His will, He does for me.

(John 15:7)

Paul goes on in Ephesians 1:18 to say, *"the eyes of your understanding being enlightened; that you may know."* Paul is praying for us to know something. He is praying for us to have revelation and wisdom in the knowledge of God. So we can know *"the hope of His calling, what are the riches of the glory of His inheritance in the saints, and what is the exceeding greatness of His power toward us who believe, according to the working of His mighty power which He worked in Christ when He raised Him from the dead"* (v. 18-20).

Why doesn't Paul just say, "I pray that the power will hit you upside the head"? If you don't understand how to walk in truth and power, what it really means is, once a church service is over you will go back out into the real world facing the same problems, and you will end up in the same negative circumstances again. What we have done is, we have tried to impart the power, but we didn't pray that they would *know* the power. Paul prays that we would *know*. Then, no matter where we are, whether the preacher is present or not, whether it is Sunday or not, whether we have our friend beside us or not, if we have the Spirit of wisdom and revelation, we will be led by the truth (God's Word).

Usually, we pray for the power to come down, but Paul prayed for us to *know* what Jesus has already done for us. It seems to me that we are always trying to get God to do something, and Paul is praying that *we would plug into what He has already done.*

RENEWAL TRUTH

The Lord has done great things for me.

(Psalm 126:2)

Paul prayed that we would know *"what is the greatness of His power toward us who believe, according to the working of His mighty power which He worked in Christ when He raised Him from the dead and seated Him at His right hand in the heavenly places"* (Ephesians 1:19-20).

That resurrection power is now ours. While we are busy begging God to send a revival, God is saying, "I sent My Son, I have poured out My Spirit, I have given you My Word, and I have sent laborers to help you understand it, but you are still waiting for something to happen. What else can I do?" We need to stop asking God to give us things He has already given!

I remember sitting in Bible school some thirty years ago. One of my teachers was talking about the days of revival in 1948, and he said, "Those days are coming back and they are going to hit us anytime." He believed revival was to hit before the 90's. I raised my hand and asked, "Do we just have to wait for it, or is there something we can do to kick start it?" He said we had to wait on God's timing. I went out and started a church that grew to five times the size of his church within two years. We went ahead and had our revival, while he was still waiting on revival to come.

This mentality needs to be replaced with the knowledge of what God has already done for us. This is what the renewal of the mind is all about. I am not waiting on God. He is waiting on me. As I am transformed by the renewing of my mind, I begin to establish the perfect will of God. I think when Jesus told the disciples how to pray, He was giving them the perspective that we must have. *"In this manner, therefore, pray: Our Father in heaven, hallowed be Your name. Your kingdom come..."* (Matthew 6:9-10).

That wasn't a question or a request. It was a demand on what God has given. "Thy Kingdom be established," not "Thy Kingdom, I'm coming." *Thy kingdom come.* Establish it. Make it happen. Put it into the lives of people on earth. Then, *"Your will be done,"* not "If it be Thy will."

Know the will of God and establish it. *"Your will be done on earth as it is in heaven"* (v. 10). Not, "I can't wait to get to heaven." No, *Your will be done on earth,* not "I can't wait until I'm out of here, man. I've got the Jonah spirit on me." If you've got Jonah's attitude, God will find you a special prayer room and it won't be comfy (like the belly of a whale)!

This attitude that Jesus is giving us is not, "The Kingdom of God is coming." His Kingdom is in us. We are to establish it and demand that the will of God be done in the earth now. I am helping people to receive this truth and establish it in their own lives. I'm not just waiting for something to hit. It has already hit! Jesus gave His life, the Holy Spirit has come, and the truth has been given. Now, go on and make it happen in your life.

Personal Application of Renewal Truths

1. I am tuning my ears to hear truth by: _____

_____

_____

_____

2. Wisdom is: _____

_____

_____

3. Revelation is: _____

_____

_____

4. My soul is prospering because: _____

_____

_____

_____

5. The result of prosperity in my mind is: _____

_____

_____

_____

7

YOUR WILL
& GOD'S WILL

Seek the Lord while He may be found, call upon Him while
He is near.

Isaiah 55:6

This Scripture infers that there will come a day when the Lord will not be found. Then verse 7 goes on to say:

Let the wicked forsake his way, and the unrighteous man
his thoughts; let him return to the Lord, and He will have
mercy on him; and to our God, for He will abundantly
pardon.

Part of the process of seeking the Lord is to forsake thoughts that do not come from righteousness. We are to renew our thoughts with God's Word to agree with what God says. In reality, you do *not return to the Lord* until you begin to forsake your own thoughts and change your thinking to agree with God's thoughts.

For My thoughts are not your thoughts, nor are your ways
My ways," says the Lord. For as the heavens are higher

YOUR UNLIMITED LIFE: Breaking Habits that Hold You Back

than the earth, so are My ways higher than your ways, and My thoughts than your thoughts.

Isaiah 55:8-9

The Lord spoke to me years ago about this passage of Scripture. He said, "When you have My thoughts, you have My ways. If you don't have My thoughts, you don't have My ways."

If we want God's ways for our children, we need His thoughts about being a parent. If we want God's ways, His blessing and His provision in our business, we must have His ways in our mind regarding business. When we have God's thoughts, we will have His ways.

When I go into a situation, I ask God to reveal to me what He is thinking about the situation; how He would have me deal with the specific issue. If I am thinking what God is thinking, I can figure out how He is going to move. When I have His thoughts, I can have His ways.

Scripture says, *"He [God] made known His ways to Moses, His acts to the children of Israel"* (Psalm 103:7). In other words, Moses knew more about God than just the miracles that He did. The people didn't want to know, they didn't plug in. Remember, the people said to Moses that they didn't want God to talk to them. They wanted Moses to talk to God and then transfer the message. They didn't want to hear God's thoughts, so they didn't know His ways.

You have to decide what kind of Christian you want to be. Do you want to see the acts of God occasionally, or are you going to be one who presses in to know His thoughts so you can know His ways? A successful Christian moves in God's ways because he [she] knows God's thoughts.

RENEWAL TRUTH

Because I know God's thoughts and His ways
through the Holy Spirit, I am strong and I am doing
great exploits to bring glory to Him.

(Daniel 11:32)

Paul said, *"But the natural man does not receive the things of the Spirit of God, for they are foolishness to him; nor can he know them, because they are spiritually discerned"* (1 Corinthians 2:14).

The natural man cannot get hold of the thoughts of God. If you think like the average guy in the world, you will never understand what God is thinking, because to know the thoughts of God, you have to think spiritually. If this seems like a completely foreign concept, don't lose heart but know that the more time spent listening and speaking with the Holy Spirit, the more you will learn to hear His guidance.

When you think in line with the Word, which is truth, you are spiritually minded and spiritually discerning. You will begin to hear, understand, and perceive the thoughts of God.

But he who is spiritual judges all things, yet he himself is rightly judged by no one. For "who has known the mind of the Lord that he may instruct Him?" But we have the mind of Christ.

1 Corinthians 2:15-16

As we become sensitive to the Spirit of God and become spiritually minded, we will begin to possess the mind of Christ. Our natural, carnal thoughts will be replaced with God's thoughts.

Perhaps you are a young man who is looking for a wife. You begin a relationship with a girl and you question if this is the right person for you. If you are spiritually minded, God's anointing will lead you and you will know. The anointing that abides in you will teach you all truth. If you are not thinking with your hormones (physical desires), like the average guy in the world, you will know whether the girl is right or not. You won't have to go to fourteen counselors and twelve pastors and take a personality test. You will know.

A problem develops when your hormones are stronger than the mind of Christ in your life. You are thinking about her perfect hair and even convince yourself she must be perfect because she serves in church. She may be completely carnally minded, but she goes to church and she is pretty.

You can't hear the anointing. You can't hear the mind of Christ on the inside of you. The anointing is trying to lead you into all truth saying, "No, no, no! This is not the woman that will help you fulfill your destiny."

RENEWAL TRUTH

The fruit of the Holy Spirit -
love, joy, peace, longsuffering,
kindness, goodness, faithfulness, gentleness,
and self-control — are maturing in my human spirit.

(Galatians 5:22-23)

You are trying to get what your natural man wants, and the natural man does not hear or receive the things of the Spirit of God because the things of the Spirit are spiritually discerned. You are not spiritually discerning, so you are missing the voice of Christ. Therefore, you don't have the thoughts or the ways of God.

Six months down the road you go to your pastor seeking counsel, either because you have gotten into a worldly relationship and you have ended up in sin, or you are hurt, let down, and discouraged. You explain, in your state of destitution, that you don't understand how this could possibly have happened to you. It happened because you didn't forsake your own thoughts and plug into God's thoughts so you could have His way in your relationship.

Each day we should seek for the higher thoughts (God's thoughts) and the higher ways of thinking. If we will do that, then we will begin to have God's way in our relationships, in our finances, in our ministry or careers, and in everything we do. Every day we are faced with a choice: Do I think the thoughts of the natural man, or do I think the thoughts of God?

The human soul is made up of the mind, will, and emotions. The things of the Spirit are eternal, and we are supernaturally affected when we are born of God. The things of the soul are naturally and gradually affected as we grow, learn, and renew the mind with the Word of God. So the will of a person must be renewed as part of the process of renewing the mind.

Paul prayed, *"Now may the God of peace Himself sanctify you completely; and may your whole spirit, soul, and body be preserved blameless at the coming of our Lord Jesus Christ"* (1 Thessalonians 5:23). The "will" is part of the soul realm, and it must be renewed and developed.

The human will is almost like a muscle. When you practice anything with your physical muscles, they learn to do things better. Soon they will do things automatically. So it is with the human will. Whatever you do over and over will begin to become automatic.

GOD GAVE MAN THE ABILITY TO "CHOOSE"

We are going to look at the will and see how it works in the negative world and in the positive world, and how we need to use our will as we develop our spiritual mind.

Let's go back to the book of beginnings, the book of Genesis. In chapter 1 God created the heavens and the earth, plant and animal life. He spoke the creation process into being. But when He came to man, He said, *"Let Us make man in Our image, according to Our likeness"* (Genesis 1:26). Something took place in the creation process that hadn't happened before. God had been creating out of His mind, out of His infinite wisdom, and out of His infinite ability. But now He says, "We are going to create something that is like Us."

"Let them [man] have dominion over the fish of the sea, over the birds of the air, and over the cattle, over all the earth and over every creeping thing that creeps on the earth." So God created man in His own image; in the image of God He created him; male and female He created

them. Then God blessed them, and God said to them, "Be fruitful and multiply; fill the earth and subdue it; have dominion."

Genesis 1:26-28

When God created Adam and Eve in His likeness and image, He gave them dominion and authority and sent them out to possess and subdue the earth. He put something in them that was not in any animal or plant. He put something in them that was unique, as we read earlier in the book, which is the will, or *the ability to choose*.

Throughout his lifetime, man makes decisions about what he is going to do and why he is going to do it. Humans ask questions, whether they like themselves, or what to do in the future. Humans get depressed and call up a friend and rant about how they hate their life, but love their new car.

Humans look at other humans and say, "Hey, wait a minute. I want to be like Mike." Or, "I want something different in my life." It might motivate you to get an education and do other things, or it may just frustrate you as you sit in your sense of victimization. But man has a will and he is aware of it. What you do with it is dependent upon how you train and develop that muscle.

Part of being created in the likeness and image of God, this divine gift of the human being, is that you get to make choices. We read in Isaiah 55:8, *"For My thoughts are not your thoughts."* You can choose to forsake your thoughts, take God's thoughts and live on a higher level, with a new way of life.

Many people don't think they can change their way of life. Some feel trapped by circumstances and what they have been told: "You are a victim." "You are white so you can't do that." "You are black so you can't go there." And on and on....

Some people will choose to fight with the union to see if they can get an extra quarter an hour. They struggle with some menial thing to see if they can improve their existence to some degree, but they don't believe that they can have a different way of living. When you grasp the fact that you can have whatever way of life you choose, then you will become a self-empowered, self-motivated individual.

A few hundred years ago, a group of people said, "We don't have to live under the bondage of a monarchy or a controlling religious system that is wicked and evil. We can choose another way of life." They packed up their goods and headed out of town. Thay went to a "new world" to make a new life because they recognized the power of their will. That has not changed. There may not be new lands for you to discover, but there is some place where you can go to do whatever you want to do, good, bad, or indifferent. You have a will, and depending on how you use it, you can have whatever way of life you want.

If you choose God's thoughts, you will get God's ways, and that is the highest level of life. That is what I am seeking after. I don't want my way. I want His way. Jesus said in Matthew 10:39 (AMP): *"Whoever finds his [lower] life will lose it [the higher life], and whoever loses his [lower] life on My account will find it [the higher life]."*

If you give up your way of thinking and take His way of

thinking, you will find a higher level of life. This is true for your marriage, for your children, your finances, your ministry or career, and for everything that you do.

God gave Adam and Eve a will and asked them to use it wisely. If they had obeyed God, they could have lived the high life. As we discussed earlier, it was the devil's deception, not his power that tripped up Adam and Eve. Neither is it merely Satan's power that is affecting Christians today. It is his deception, lies, trickery, subtleties, and cunning ways. When Adam and Eve began to think the thoughts of the devil, they lost their relationship with God. By a "choice" of their will, they were separated from Him.

What kind of existence do you want? Do you desire: life or death, blessing or cursing, positive or negative, joy or depression, prosperity or poverty, sickness or health? It is your choice. I am convinced that most people feel like they are caught up in a whirlwind, they are being carried along, and they really can't help it or change anything. But the fact is, *you can make a choice to live a higher level of life in Christ.*

Let's assume a little boy is raised up in a poor part of town. His dad and mom are just trying to keep the bills paid. He is confronted with drugs, sex, and crime every day of his life. Although he is under some terrific negative influences, *he still has a choice* to make as to whether he will be a part of it or not. This is not a rags-to-riches story of physical wealth, although that is part of the deal. This is a rags-to-riches story of the mind—a promise from God that if you choose to think different you will inevitably be choosing a better life - your unlimited life.

111

Another case in point: I know several ministers who were raised in drugs, sickness, poverty, and sin, but today they are preaching the Gospel. I know a pastor, who at seven years of age, watched as his mom was shot to death in a dope deal. Today he is preaching the Gospel. His first seven years of life were with a single parent in the midst of the worst kind of sin and degradation. At seven, with no parent, he tried to survive. As a young man he sought the Lord, changed his choices, was born of God, and is now a minister. He is affecting thousands of lives around his community, his church, and the nation through his teaching and his witness. To me, this is proof that *life is choice.*

He could have stayed where he was and said, "I can't help it. My mamma was shot when I was seven. I was raised in sin and crime. What do you expect?" I expect you to choose to get out! "I can't help it." Yes, you can because *you are created in the likeness and image of God.* He has set before you life and death, blessing and cursing. *You* choose which one you are going to have. Every person has this choice.

An Infusion of Hope in My Life

I was raised without the knowledge of God. I believed in God, but I had no knowledge of God or His Word. At thirteen years of age, I was drinking, smoking pot, and using drugs. I was trying to have fun. I figured life existed so I could get high, have fun, and if I died high, then I would die good!

After a couple of jobs as the dish washer at Denny's, the car washer at a local dealership, and the Spanaway drug dealer, I was nineteen and I was burnt out. It didn't work. Nothing I tried had worked at making me forget my problems or find happiness. Nothing was producing the kind of life I wanted. I ended up in jail too many times to count and was all messed up with drugs, crime, and depression. I was confronted with life and death, blessing and cursing. A man told me that I could continue to be the way I was, or I could choose something different. I chose, *"Whoever calls on the name of the Lord shall be saved"* (Romans 10:13).

How You Live Is Your Choice

The divine gift of choosing how you will live can be buried in such thoughts as:

- I am a victim.
- I can't help it.
- It's my circumstances.
- It's my age.
- It's my race.

Under all of these lies is a divine gift that makes you like God, with a will to choose life or death, blessing or cursing, poverty or prosperity, sickness or health. You have the privilege of making a choice.

The secular world tries to escape the reality that man has a will. They blame genetics, the environment, or the government. The truth is, each of us is who we are because of our choices.

You are not a heroin addict because of genetics or hormones. You are a heroin addict because of your choices. You are not an alcoholic because of your hormones, genetics, or anything else.

You are an alcoholic by choice. You may think some people become alcoholics easier than others, but that doesn't take away the choice required to follow that lifestyle. Some people gain weight easier than others, but we still make choices in diet and exercise.

If we were to turn back your life, we would find where relationships with others have affected and influenced you in such a way that your choices have caused you to become carnal. That doesn't mean you are a wicked, evil, negative person. It just means you made choices to end up in a very dangerous lifestyle.

Your "will" affects every area of life. Joshua said:

And if it seems evil to you to serve the Lord, choose for yourselves this day whom you will serve, whether the gods which your fathers served that were on the other side of the River, or the gods of the Amorites, in whose land you dwell. But as for me and my house, we will serve the Lord.

Joshua 24:15

In modern society, we want to hope everything works out okay based on genetics and the environmental influence. Joshua says, *it is your choice*. Our lives reveal our choices.

MARY MADE A CHOICE

Remember when Jesus went into a certain village and paid a visit to the home of Mary and Martha? While Mary made a choice to sit at Jesus' feet and hear the Word, Martha was caught up in natural preparations. Let's read this account in Luke 10:38-42:

Now it happened as they went that He entered a certain village; and a certain woman named Martha welcomed Him into her house. And she had a sister called Mary, who also sat at Jesus' feet and heard His word. But Martha was distracted with much serving, and she approached Him and said, "Lord, do You not care that my sister has left me to serve alone? Therefore tell her to help me." And Jesus answered and said to her, "Martha, Martha."

When the Lord says any word twice, you are in trouble! *"Martha, Martha, you are worried and troubled about many things"* (v. 41).

Martha was exclaiming that her problems were that Mary wouldn't help her. Jesus then explains that it's not her problem. She had a whole bunch of other problems. Jesus says, "You have piled up things in your life that have distracted, depressed, and worried you. Mary is *not* your problem. You are troubled about many things." Then Jesus says, *"But one thing is needed, and Mary has chosen that good part, which will not be taken away from her"* (v. 42).

Here is a microcosm of human will in operation. Mary chose to sit at Jesus' feet and hear His Word. Martha chose many thoughts, attitudes, and behaviors that were troubling her. She complains about the condition of her life, and Jesus highlights Mary's choice, and that it is not going to be taken away from her. In other words, "Now Martha, it is time for you to make a choice and deal with those things that are troubling your life."

RENEWAL TRUTH

My first priority in life
is to seek God's Kingdom and
His righteousness.
(Matthew 6:33)

Complaining to God about your life won't change anything. That's why when we pray negative, whiny, complaining prayers, and wonder why nothing happens, we are inadvertently crippling ourselves. What did you ask for? "I told God how I felt. I told Him I didn't need anyone. Doesn't He understand?" God answered your prayer. He just nodded His head at how miserable you are. Whining and complaining to God won't change a thing. You have chosen to be the way you are and where you are. When you start saying, "Lord, I am going to make some new choices," God says, "Now I can get involved."

"Lord, I believe I am healed in the name of Jesus." Jesus responds, "I can confirm that" (1 Peter 2:24; Isaiah 53:5).

"Lord, I am prospering and getting out of debt." God says, "I can get involved in that" (Joshua 1:8; Psalm 1:1-3).

"The joy of the Lord is my strength. No more depression for me!" The Lord responds, "I can confirm that" (Nehemiah 8:10; Isaiah 54:14-17).

Now God has something to work with because you are starting to change and make godly choices. As long as you are just complaining about your circumstances, the Lord says the same thing to you as He said to Martha. "Lord, I am having a bad day. Don't You know how my boss treats me?" The Lord says, "Martha, Martha, it's not only your boss, you have many things that you are troubled about." Mary has chosen. She made a choice. Mary is sitting at Jesus' feet, hearing the Word, and Martha is worried and troubled, all because of choices.

Paul's Choice

For to me, to live is Christ, and to die is gain. But if I live on in the flesh, this will mean fruit from my labor; yet what I shall choose I cannot tell.

Philippians 1:21-22

Paul is explaining here that to live is okay, but to die in Christ is better. We are going to have to choose. If I stay and continue to preach, teach, and minister, it will produce fruit for the Kingdom and for this earthly life. Paul realized the value of man's choice. He understood the gift God was giving to us when He allowed us to choose.

Yet what I shall choose I cannot tell. For I am hard-pressed between the two, having a desire to depart and be with Christ, which is far better. Nevertheless to remain in the flesh is more needful for you.

Philippians 1:22-24

Think of it. Here is a guy who is so developed in his relation-

117

ship with God and in his control of his own will, he says, "Man, I would like to go and be with the Lord right now."

In 2 Timothy 4:7, Paul says, *"I have fought the good fight, I have finished the race, I have kept the faith."* In other words, "I have done what the Lord has asked me to do." So now he is saying to the Philippians, "I would be better off to go be with Jesus. It is a whole lot better than hanging around here. But to stay and minister, teach, and preach would be good for you."

And being confident of this, I know that I shall remain and continue with you for your progress and joy of faith.
Philippians 1:25

Paul is writing, "I have made up my mind I am going to stay and keep ministering for your joy in the faith." In other words, "I will remain." He made a choice, an act of his will.

The model we see in the New Testament is not one of a rushed life. The Lord is not trying to quickly return, and take us up to heaven so we can get out of the mess that is earth, and enjoy the perfection that is heaven. The New Testament pattern is that of people serving humanity and loving people until the very end of our life. Recognizing the importance of our role on earth is crucial to our success. My wife Wendy always says, "Earth life is short, heaven life is long." We have the task of making the time count— getting our mind right and choosing God's plan over our own.

It's time to quit waiting on the rapture bus and get on with what God wants you to do with your life. You have been given the necessary tools. You have the Word and the power to use it for the process of shifting the way you think to the way God thinks. It is now time to receive a higher level of life for yourself as you walk in the perfect will of God. Receive your unlimited life. Start today.

Personal Application of Renewal Truths

1. Unlike animals who live by instinct, I live by:_____

   _____

   _____

   _____

   _____

   _____

2. The highest level of life for me is: _____

   _____

   _____

   _____

   _____

   _____

   _____

3. I can achieve a higher level of life by: _____

   _____

   _____

   _____

   _____

   _____

   _____

4. Some of the challenges I am facing right now, along with the Scriptures I am using to make godly choices in each situation, are:

Challenge	Scripture
_____	_____
_____	_____
_____	_____
_____	_____
_____	_____
_____	_____

5. Like Paul, it is my desire to be a "servant" to others by:

_____

_____

_____

_____

_____

_____

_____

_____

_____

_____

_____

_____

_____

_____

7924157R0

Made in the USA
Charleston, SC
22 April 2011